Rajasthan Priorities

Analysing costs and benefits

About Rajasthan Priorities

The Rajasthan Priorities project is part of the larger India Consensus – a partnership between Tata Trusts and the Copenhagen Consensus Center, which works to identify, analyse, rank and disseminate the best solutions for Indian states. The prioritization project unites the best academic research, employing cost-benefit analysis, with sector expert input, broad and inclusive stakeholder engagement, and extensive policy outreach, to evaluate and prioritise the smartest interventions.

For more information on the project, including the content of this book, please visit www.rajasthanpriorities.com.

About Tata Trusts

Tata Trusts is amongst India's oldest, non-sectarian philanthropic organisations. The Trusts own two-third of the stock holding of Tata Sons, the apex company of the Tata group of companies. The wealth that accrues from this asset supports an assortment of causes, institutions and individuals in a wide variety of areas. In this manner, the profits that the Tata companies earn go back many times over to the communities they operate in. These funds have been deployed towards a whole range of community development programmes across the country, for over 100 years.

About Copenhagen Consensus Center

The Copenhagen Consensus Center is an award-winning think tank that researches the smartest solutions for the world's biggest problems and has helped policy-makers and philanthropists how to spend their money most effectively. Copenhagen Consensus has helped to focus billions of dollars of global aid and development spending on smarter priorities. The world's oldest academic publisher, Cambridge University Press, has published seven volumes of the Center's research.

RAJASTHAN PRIORITIES

ANALYSING COSTS AND BENEFITS

BY

BJORN LOMBORG

MANORAMA BAKSHI

RAJASTHAN PRIORITIES AN INDIA CONSENSUS PRIORITIZATION PROJECT

COPENHAGEN
CONSENSUS
CENTER

info@copenhagenconsensus.com
www.copenhagenconsensus.com

Cover design by: Rick Szuecs Design rickszuecs.com
Graphs and figures made with infogram.com, data source is the project research paper analyzing the respective interventions.

This work has been produced as a part of the Rajasthan Priorities project under the larger, India Consensus project.

This project is undertaken in partnership with Tata Trusts.

TATA TRUSTS

Please cite the work as follows: Lomborg and Bakshi, Rajasthan Priorities - analysing costs and benefits, Copenhagen Consensus Center and Tata Trusts 2019.

ISBN 978-1-940003-21-4

Contents

FOREWORD

BY RATAN N. TATA

For more than one hundred years, Tata Trusts have played a pioneering role in empowering, enabling, and transforming communities across India.

Through grant-making, direct implementation and co-partnership strategies, the Trusts support and drive innovation in areas as important as healthcare and nutrition; water and sanitation; energy; education; rural livelihoods; natural resource management; urban poverty alleviation; enhancing civil society and governance; media, arts, crafts and culture; and diversified employment.

Founder Jamsetji Tata's vision of proactive philanthropy is just as relevant today as it was a century ago, ensuring that the Trusts catalyse societal development with initiatives and interventions that have a contemporary relevance to the nation.

Today, spread over 17 states and 170 districts across the country, programmes supported by the Trusts reach out to millions of households through an efficient network of more than 450 partner organisations. Additionally, the Trusts' projects and initiatives, especially in the area of educational attainment, significantly contribute to capacity building across the country.

The Tata Trusts' collaboration with Copenhagen Consensus Center on the India Consensus project, which Rajasthan Priorities is part of, is one of the ways that we are providing support for the development of innovation and intellectual capital, at the state level.

State governments are vital partners for Tata Trusts. Consolidated state government expenditure is now around 1.4 times the size of the Central government expenditure. With vision and judicious spending, states have the financial muscle to play a major role in the transformation of communities.

Given the breadth and diversity of India, every region has its own complexities, challenges, and opportunities, so solutions to challenges must be developed at a local level. But this does not mean that there is no role for world-class expertise or input.

The expectations placed upon state governments in this nation (and indeed on every state and national government in the world) are growing ever-greater. Quite rightly, citizens everywhere in the world demand better schooling and infrastructure, cleaner environment, and better-quality healthcare. Especially in the world's largest democracy, where free speech and free exchange are enshrined, these voices are powerful and important.

Indeed, for political decision-makers, one of the most important and weighty tasks is listening to the many different civic groups, looking closely at the challenges and opportunities ahead, and deciding carefully how and where to allocate limited resources.

No government or organisation on Earth is capable of meeting every last demand from citizens. The allocation of scarce resources can only be improved when decision-makers and the populace are provided with better information about spending choices.

This, indeed, is the starting point of the India Consensus project. This comprehensive undertaking provides a wealth of new economic findings, presented in this book, establishing what various interventions and initiatives can achieve in the state of Rajasthan.

The benefits of the project are manifold, but the initiative particularly supports the Tata Trust's approach of fostering both innovation and intellectual capital.

The Trusts have long focused on innovative technologies and approaches to enhance the quality of life of communities. The focus has been on bringing in high-quality talent and technologies to speed and scale up interventions.

Tata Trusts have partnered with premier educational and technical institutions around the world, and like-minded multinationals, to design, develop and implement innovative programmes across different sectors such as education, digital literacy, health, livelihoods, and more.

The approach undertaken by Rajasthan Priorities is entirely aligned with this approach: it is cutting edge analysis. It is particularly innovative to apply cost-benefit analysis across such a broad range of different spending options, at a state level. Very few governments or organisations undertake this important work, because it is so complex.

Therefore, this approach itself breaks new ground, by standardising the academic approaches and ensuring that the costs and benefits of various policies can cohesively be understood together.

The contribution that Rajasthan Priorities makes to boosting intellectual capacity is just as important to Tata Trusts. As Jamsetji Tata once said, "What advances a nation or a community is not so much to prop up its weakest and most helpless members, but to lift up the best and the most gifted, so as to make them of the greatest service to the country."

Some of the finest specialist economists from India have contributed academically to this project, giving their own service to the cause of identifying the social costs and benefits of various different approaches to challenges.

The findings of the Eminent Panel, published in this book, are a particularly important contribution because they highlight how thought leaders from India find that this research can be understood and interpreted, in ways that can lead to better decision-making. This contribution can only lead to a richer and more vibrant public discourse.

While the project has produced a wealth of innovative and informative findings, it is what happens next that is very important.

In that regard, this book is the opening of a conversation, rather than the end of one. The understandings between Rajasthan Priorities and the state government has great potential to help translate this research and apply it in ways that will have a very important impact and will actually help to transform communities in effective ways. This would indeed be an enduring legacy of this project.

Mumbai, 23rd October, 2018

CONTRIBUTORS

Dr Bjorn Lomborg is president of the Copenhagen Consensus Center and visiting professor at Copenhagen Business School. The Copenhagen Consensus Center is a think-tank that researches the smartest ways to do good. For this work, Lomborg was named one of TIME magazine's 100 most influential people in the world. His numerous books include "The Skeptical Environmentalist", "Cool It", "How to Spend $75 Billion to Make the World a Better Place" and "The Nobel Laureates' Guide to the Smartest Targets for the World 2016-2030." In 2016, Prospect Magazine awarded Copenhagen Consensus Center, US International Affairs Think Tank of the Year.

Dr Manorama Bakshi is Senior Advisor, Outreach and partnerships for the India Consensus Project. She is a development professional with over 20+ years of experience in strategic planning and partnerships, policy advocacy, media and communications, program formulation and management with major focus on public health. She is skilled in building and nurturing partnerships with government, development partners, private sector, civil society organizations. She has worked as a senior technical officer at MOHFW and on projects with UNDP, ILO and USAID projects. She has been giving lectures at various Universities/Management and forums like CII, PHD chamber of commerce and is visiting faculty to management institutes. She is author of 'HIV/AIDS policy guidelines for the Corporates'. Drafted guidelines on HIV/AIDS for Corporates, hospitality sector and for Ministry of Health. As a freelance she has been writing in various newspapers and journals and has a special feature, "Connecting with my very own" coming out every month in Naad, a Kashmiri monthly magazine.

Thank you to all economists and experts who contributed to the academic research on costs and benefits under the leadership of **Dr Brad Wong** the Chief Economist of Copenhagen Consensus Center, and a specialist in social, economic and environmental benefit-cost analysis across development sectors.

The dedicated and enthusiastic India Consensus team consists of Amar Chancal, Dr. Paola Grenier, Steffi Itola, David Lessmann, Roland Mathiasson, Dr. BM Naidu, Dr. Saleema Razvi, Kuldeep Singh, Tejbir Singh and David Young with particular acknowledgement to the support provided by Pooja Parvati at Tata Trusts.

Panel of Eminent Economists

The Eminent Panel members met and put questions to the researchers at a three-day academic conference in Jaipur, Rajasthan, in June 2018. The Eminent Panel comprises:

Dr Bibek Debroy is Chairman of the Economic Advisory Council to the Prime Minister (EAC-PM) and Member of NITI Aayog, the think-tank of the Indian Government. Dr. Bibek Debroy was educated in Ramakrishna Mission School, Narendrapur; Presidency College, Kolkata; Delhi School of Economics and Trinity College, Cambridge. He was awarded the 'Padma Shri' (the fourth-highest civilian honour in India) in 2015. In 2016, he was awarded the Lifetime Achievement Award by US-India Business Summit. He has worked in following Professional bodies: Presidency College, Kolkata (1979-83); Gokhale Institute of Politics and Economics, Pune (1983-87); Indian Institute of Foreign Trade, Delhi (1987-93); as The Director of a Ministry of Finance/UNDP project on legal reforms (1993-98); Department of Economic Affairs (1994-95); National Council of Applied Economic Research (1995-96); Rajiv Gandhi Institute for Contemporary Studies (1997-2005); PHD Chamber of Commerce and Industry (2005-06); Centre for Policy Research (2007-2015).He has authored/edited several books, papers and popular articles and has also been a Consulting/Contributing Editor with several newspapers.

Professor Amitabh Mattoo is Advisor to the Chief Minister of Jammu and Kashmir, with the status of a Cabinet Minister; CEO and Honorary Director of the Australia India Institute at Delhi; and Professor of International Relations at the University of Melbourne. He is also a Professor of Disarmament Studies in Jawaharlal Nehru University. He has been a member of the National Security Advisory Board and a member of the National Knowledge Commission to the Prime Minister of India. Professor Amitabh Mattoo was Vice-Chancellor of the University of Jammu from 2002-2008. Recognizing his contribution to education and public life, the President of India honoured Professor Mattoo with the Padma Shri, one of India's highest civilian awards.

Dr Alok Ray is Former Professor of Economics, Indian Institute of Management Calcutta, India where he taught for more than 30 years. He obtained his PhD from University of Rochester, USA. Prof. Ray has also taught at Calcutta University, Delhi School of Economics, Cornell University (USA), University of Rochester (USA), University of Pittsburg (USA), Portland State University (USA), Queen's University (Canada) and Monash University (Melbourne, Australia). He is the author of a book: Trade, Protection and Economic Policy (Macmillan) and many professional articles in leading international journals. In addition, he writes regular columns on contemporary issues in several English dailies. Professor Ray has been a consultant to United Nations, World Bank, Government of India and a number of private sector companies. He is a recipient of the prestigious V.K.R.V. Rao Award in Economics for his research contributions and the "Best Teacher of Economics" Award by Bengal Economic Association.

Dr Rathin Roy is Director and CEO of the National Institute of Public Finance and Policy New Delhi; and Member, Economic Advisory Council to the Prime Minister of India. With postings in London, New York, Kathmandu, Brasilia and Bangkok, he has worked as an Economic Diplomat and Policy Advisor with UNDP, focusing on emerging economies. He has taught at the Universities of Manchester and London and served as Economic Adviser with the Thirteenth Finance Commission and as a Member, Seventh Central Pay Commission, Government of India. Dr. Roy is Member, India Advisory Committee, United Nations Environment Programme (UNEP) Inquiry into a Sustainable Financial System, Member on the Meta Council on Inclusive Growth, World Economic Forum, Geneva, Member on FRBM Review Committee, Government of India. Dr. Roy's policy interests and publications have mainly focused on fiscal and macroeconomic issues pertinent to human development in developing and emerging economies. Dr. Roy has written extensively on fiscal space for human development, inter-government fiscal issues, fiscal marksmanship, macro-economic conditionality and IMF Article-IV policy analyses. Dr. Roy holds a Ph.D in Economics from the University of Cambridge, an MA in Economics from the Jawaharlal Nehru University and a BA (Hons) in Economics from St. Stephen's College, University of Delhi.

ACADEMIC RESEARCHERS

Abhishek Kumar, CUG, Gandhinagar
Abusaleh Shariff, US-India Policy Inst.
Amitabh Kundu, RIS, New Delhi
Amitendu Palit, NU Singapore
Anandajit Goswami, TERI
Amit Sharma, The World Bank
Arjun Kumar, IHD, New Delhi
Bjorn Larsen, Ind. Consultant
Bhawna Tyagi, IL&FS
D K Mangal, IIHMR, Jaipur
Dinesh Kumar, IRAP, Hyderabad
Eshita Mukherjee, DEF
Gagan Nigam, IL&FS
Gaurav Bhatiani, IL&FS
Harsha Meenawat, IL&FS
Kaushik Bandyopadhyay, IIM, Lucknow
Kushal Sagar Prakash, Sunay Policy
Manish Gupta, PDCOR
Mansi Arora, Sunay Policy Advisory
Md Mahbub Hossain, IIHMR, Jaipur
Michael Murigi, Uni. of Sydney
Mrinal Chadha, NU Ireland
Munshi Sulaiman, Save the Children International
Nata Duvvury, NU Ireland
Neeraj Sharma, IIHMR, Jaipur
Nilanjan Banik, Bennett Uni., Delhi
Nim Pathy, Imperial College London
Nirupama Soundararajan, PIF
PR Sodani, IIHMR, Jaipur
Priyesh Shukla, PDCOR
Rajesh Chakrabarti, Sunay Policy Adv.
Reena Mithal, Sankhya Capital
Ritu Srivastava, DEF
S D Gupta, IIHMR, Jaipur
S V Subramanian, Harvard T.H. Chan School of Public Health
Shagun Khurana, Pahle India
Shreelata Rao Seshadri, Azim Premji University
Sonali Chowdhry, IL&FS y
SouvikBhattacharjya, TERI
Srinivas Raghavendra, NU Ireland
Surabhi Mittal, TARINA, TCI
Vijayalakshmi Hebbare, CGHR, Bangalore
William Joe, IEG, Delhi

ACADEMIC ADVISORY COMMITTEE

Dr Jyoti Kiran is an economist & academician of national repute trained at premier institutes like, the University of Rajasthan, Delhi School of Economics and the University of Huddersfield (UK). A PhD in Economics and a specialist on employment, development policy and finance, she has researched and written extensively on economic policy and development. One of her major specializations lies in Economics of Urban Development and she has worked extensively on Urban Finance. She taught at reputed institutes like NIT Nagpur for about 13 years and later worked in leadership positions in management institutes as Dean and Director.

Professor Vijay Shankar Vyas is Professor Emeritus in the Institute of Development Studies, Jaipur, and has a Ph.D degree in Economics from the University of Bombay. Prof. Vyas served as Director of the Agro-Economic Research Centre, Vallabh Vidyanagar; Professor of Economics and Dean of Faculty of Humanities and Social Sciences, Sardar Patel University; Member, Agricultural Prices Commission of the Government of India; Director, Indian Institute of Management, Ahmedabad; Senior Advisor in the Department of Agriculture and Rural Development of the World Bank, Washington, D.C. He was a Senior Fellow of the IDRC, Canada, and a Visiting Scholar at the South Asia Centre of the Boston University, U.S.A.

Shri C. S. Rajan is Deputy Chairman of the Chief Ministers Advisory Council, Government of Rajasthan and was Chief Secretary, Government of Rajasthan from 2014 to 2016. Shri Rajan is a 1978 batch Indian Administrative Service officer and has served in several key positions in the Government. He was Additional Chief Secretary- Infrastructure, ACS Rural Development and Panchayat Raj, Principal Secretary, Industries, Pr. Secy. Energy, Pr. Secy. Public Works, Secretary Agriculture etc. for long periods. Shri Rajan has led many reforms and has been a key person in the Rajasthan Government on development planning and implementation of socio-economic policies and schemes in the State.

Mr Pradeep S Mehta is the founder Secretary General of the Jaipur-based Consumer Unity & Trust Society (CUTS International), a leading economic policy research, advocacy and networking, non-governmental group in India, with offices in Nairobi, Lusaka, Hanoi, Accra and Geneva. CUTS was established in 1983 and has completed 30 glorious years. In April 2012, Mehta has been nominated to the High-Level Stakeholders Panel of WTO on Defining the Future of Trade. He serves on several policy-making bodies of the Government of India and Inter-Governmental Organisations related to trade, investment, competition, environment and consumer affairs.

Professor S.D.Gupta is an Public Health expert with a distinguished academic and research career. He is a fellow of Indian Association of Preventive & Social Medicine, and a long-term member of the International Epidemiological

INTRODUCTION

BY BJORN LOMBORG AND SHIREEN VAKIL

Businesses, civil society and, indeed, every citizen has a stake in the important budget-setting process, which sees roughly 1,71,300 crore rupees allocated among important causes.

With a diversified economy, high growth rates, and an international high profile, Rajasthan is an important part of India's success story. But Rajasthan, like every state and nation on Earth, does not have unlimited funds. It has to choose between many worthy opportunities to speed progress and respond to the remaining challenges.

What is the best way to continue developing while ensuring that everyone benefits, and gaps are closed? There are nearly as many different answers to that question as there are people living in the state.

For many, education is paramount – but does that mean first focusing on getting more people into tertiary education, or improving early childhood access, or on expanding skills training programs?

For others, the place to start is infrastructure. Some argue that health problems or social ills should be solved before tackling anything else. For yet others, the priority is strengthening institutions.

With finite resources, it is important for every decision-maker – not just in Rajasthan but in every state and national government – to ask him or herself, how much will we achieve by spending that extra rupee on this policy or that? For example, what will we achieve by focusing on helping more people into higher education, and how much good will we achieve for Rajasthan from spending the same amount on early childhood education? What social dividends will we reap from focusing on eliminating rural extreme poverty, and what will we achieve if we invest in expanding health packages?

Finding answers to these questions means creating knowledge and data that lifts the discourse and can lead to improved allocation of scarce resources.

Tata Trusts, one of the oldest non-sectarian philanthropic organisations, has been working with the think tank, the Copenhagen Consensus Center, to provide this very data. We have worked with many of Rajasthan's top thinkers and influencers, including hundreds of sector experts, to find a wide range of views about the state's biggest challenges and most constructive responses.

Copenhagen Consensus has previously carried out research projects looking at global development priorities as well as national spending choices in Bangladesh and in Haiti. Our research– undertaken by some of the world's top economists, including Nobel laureates – has been used to inform the choices of UN agencies, philanthropic organisations, and governments.

By focusing on where we can achieve the most benefits, we can help decision-makers with the difficult task of priority-setting. Of course, cost-benefit analysis is not the only thing they should pay attention to – but it is a vital input.

The idea is to capture not only those that are 'hot' issues on the political agenda, but also to identify areas which might get less publicity – but where added focus could help to achieve a lot.

Encouragingly, there has been a lot of enthusiasm in Rajasthan for the idea of cost-benefit analysis as a way to set priorities.

This project began with engagement across the state's vibrant policy, civil sector and academic circles.

We engaged with more than 430 sector experts across Rajasthan through a series of 18 sector expert consultations. The sector experts were from the government, donors, academia, NGOs, and think tanks. These consultations created a rare opportunity to extract an in-depth and nuanced overview of the challenges facing Rajasthan. These consultations resulted in over 880 policy interventions, from health, education and food security to clean water access, environmental preservation, climate change, and infrastructure. The ideas from these discussions were added to the pool of research topics. The proposed interventions were then shortlisted and reviewed by the Rajasthan Academic Advisory Committee, who agreed on a final list of 85 interventions to be researched and evaluated using cost-benefit analysis.

We then worked with some of the state's – and India's – top economists to analyze both the costs and the social benefits for each of these policies. In this booklet, much of their research is described.

Full copies of each of the research papers can be found and downloaded for free on the Rajasthan Priorities website. In this book, each chapter tells its own story about opportunities to speed progress and continue to respond to challenges.

At the end of this book, are the findings of the Rajasthan Priorities Eminent Panel, Dr Bibek Debroy, Professor Amitabh Mattoo, Dr Alok Ray, and Dr Rathin Roy.

They gathered and interviewed all of the researchers and deliberated over the research, before agreeing on a list of the most effective investments. It is our hope that the research studies and eminent panel findings can provide inspiration for debate, and a valuable policy-making input.

None of this would have been possible without the hard work of the India Consensus team led by and Dr Paola Grenier, Pooja Parvati, and Dr Brad Wong in bringing this project to its logical conclusion. Dr Manorama Bakshi along with the other team members Amar Chancal, Steffi Itola, David Lessmann, Roland Mathiasson, Dr. BM Naidu, Dr. Saleema Razvi, Kuldeep Singh, Tejbir Singh and David Young did a phenomenal job in accomplishing results in a timely manner. A special note of gratitude to the state team of Tata Trusts in Rajasthan led by Malika Srivastava who supported and facilitated the entire process.

There has already been a very promising response from the state government to whom we presented these findings and requested each department to take up 4-5 recommendations. Most promising is the fact that Principal Secretary issued a Circular, sharing the research findings and outlining the purpose of the project. The Circular requested that recipients "examine the said reports and intimate the future course of action at the earliest", and informed recipients of the Hon'ble Chief Minister's directive that departments should examine the findings, and incorporate relevant findings into Annual Action Plans.

Ensuring that this work is of maximum use for Rajasthan is exactly what we have set out to work on, since the Eminent Panel met. And in providing these findings in book form, we hope that our conversation can broaden and help to ensure that thousands of crores of extra rupees of good can be created by virtue of sharpening the focus on the very best policies. This will ensure that more money and attention is devoted to the policies and interventions that will help Rajasthan to write a bold new chapter in its admirable success story.

OVERVIEW OF THE SOCIAL, ECONOMIC AND ENVIRONMENTAL VALUE PER RUPEE SPENT

SOCIAL, ECONOMIC AND ENVIRONMENTAL
BENEFITS FOR EVERY RUPEE SPENT

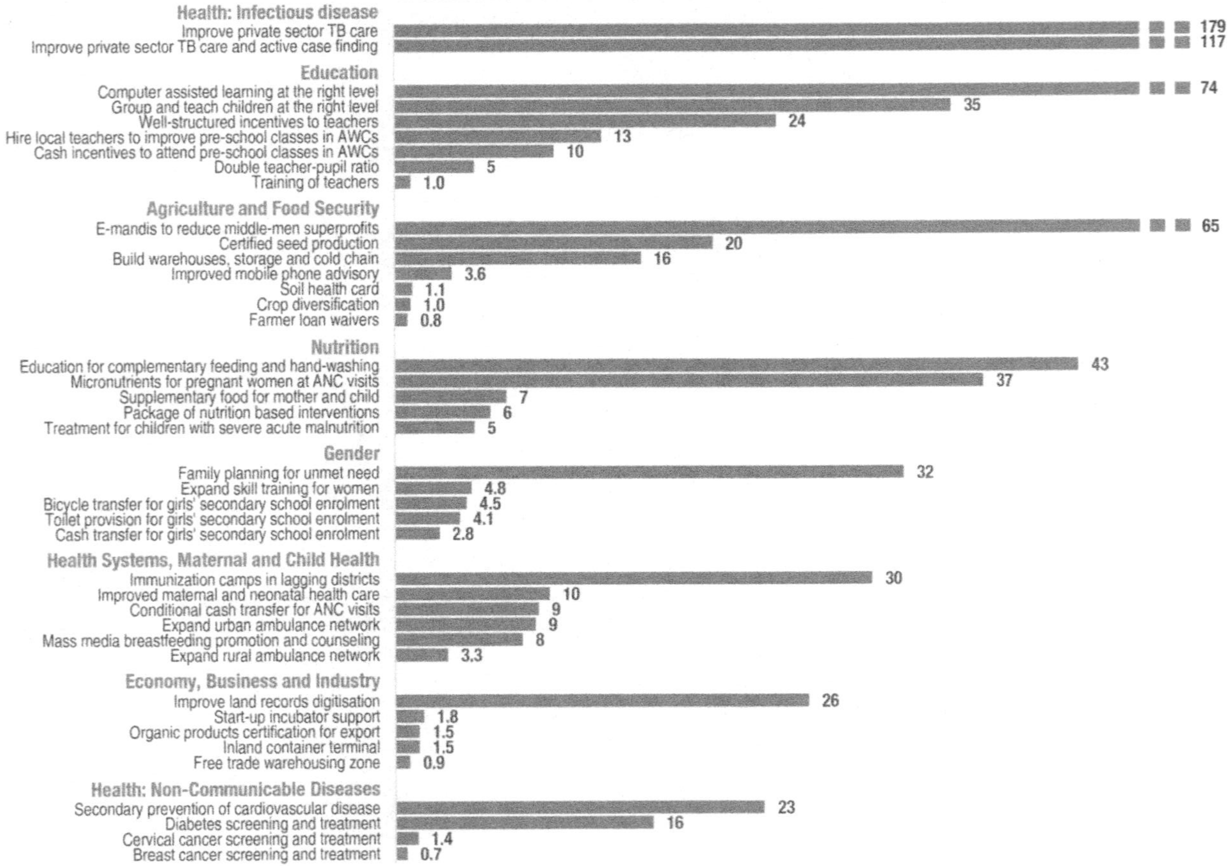

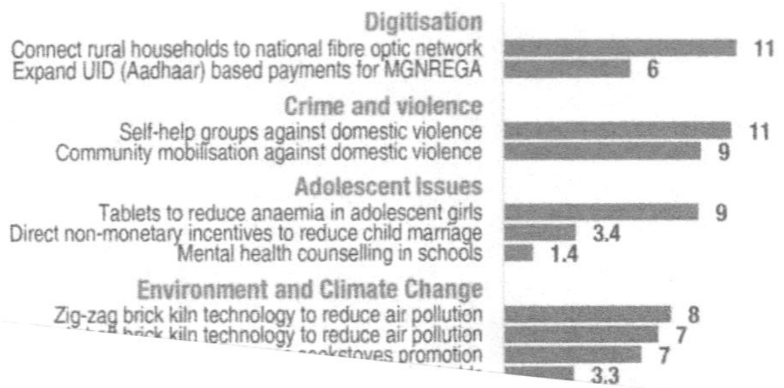

Digitisation
Connect rural households to national fibre optic network
11
Expand UID (Aadhaar) based payments for MGNREGA
6
Crime and violence
Self-help groups against domestic violence
11
Community mobilisation against domestic violence
9
Adolescent Issues
Tablets to reduce anaemia in adolescent girls
9
Direct non-monetary incentives to reduce child marriage
3.4
Mental health counselling in schools
1.4
Environment and Climate Change
Zig-zag brick kiln technology to reduce air pollution
8
brick kiln technology to reduce air pollution
7
cookstoves promotion
7
3.3

ADOLESCENT MENTAL HEALTH: AN UNDERESTIMATED MENACE

Fifteen crore people in India are in need of mental health interventions and care, yet mental health is seldom part of the conversation on public priorities. Early intervention is particularly important: globally 10 to 20 percent of children and adolescents experience mental health disorders, and three-quarters of all mental illnesses emerge by the mid-20s.

Whilst the importance of physical health of adolescents, especially adolescent girls has been gaining ground in recent years, mental health remains a neglected and often taboo area.

Researchers SD Gupta, Md Mahbub Hossain, Neeraj Sharma, PR Sodani, and DK Mangal from IIHMR University, Jaipur, note that a lack of awareness about mental health often means that people do not access the services that they need, and only those patients with severe mental disorders are diagnosed and treated.

Untreated mental health conditions in adolescence can carry forward and worsen. It is extremely important to identify signs of trauma or disturbance and offer adequate counselling before these develop into a more serious condition requiring medication. Abuse and violence often cause trauma and mental health conditions, and evidence shows that domestic violence for instance is one of the strongest predictors of suicide amongst girls.

While there are gaps in the evidence on adolescent mental health, the 2016 National Mental Health Survey of India showed mental disorders among 7.3 percent of children aged 13-17, with prevalence in urban metros nearly double (13.5 percent) that of rural areas (6.9 percent). Major illnesses include depressive disorders (2.6 percent), disabilities affecting intellectual status (1.7 percent), agoraphobia (2.3 percent), autism (1.6 percent), psychotic disorders (1.3 percent) and phobic anxiety disorders (1.3 percent). Early recognition and intervention can improve outcomes.

Mental disorders in the age group 13-17

The researchers propose a screening, referral and treatment intervention for classes VI to XII at private and public schools, roughly covering children aged 11-17. Participation would be voluntary, requiring the consent of the adolescent and their parent or guardian.

Costs would include human resources for screening, material development and dissemination, along with clinical assessment, linkage to specialized care providers, and mental health services. In Rajasthan, assuming that 80% of adolescents took part, enrolment and screening would would cost about ₹189 crores annually.

It is reasonably expected to stop some young deaths from self-harm each year – but mental Health also adversely affects the learning, education and social development of children. Interventions on this front would therefore also considerably reduce mental and physical disability, meaning that people can lead more fruitful, productive lives, and contribute more to society, including economically. The authors calculate that, put into monetary terms, all these benefits are worth ₹264 crores to the Rajasthan economy.

Investment in adolescent mental health not only 'breaks even' but is a solid investment and generates returns to society worth nearly one-and-a-half rupees for every rupee spent.

Adolescent physical health is also crucial, and the researchers highlight the benefits from focusing on anaemia, which affects many Indian girls.

Iron deficiency reduces physical fitness, which affects academic performance. In the long run, this affects maternal and child health and further increases the burden of disease.

A notable measure to address this challenge across India among 10-19 year-olds is the Weekly Iron and Folic Acid Supplementation which includes supervised consumption of iron and folic acid supplements with biannual deworming medications.

Anaemia cases averted due to the proposed intervention

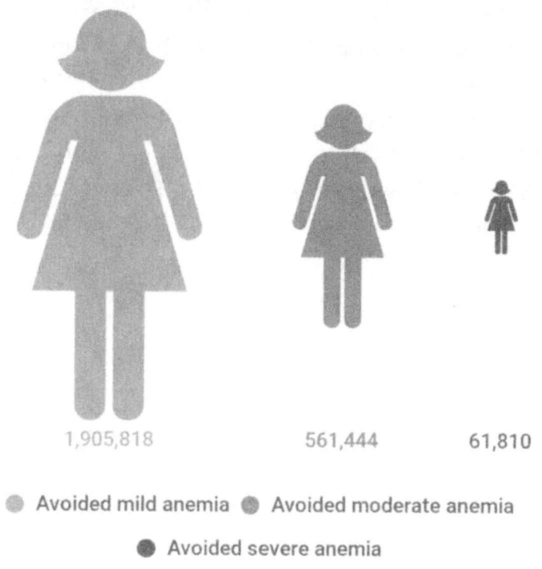

The researchers conduct a cost-benefit analysis for a program similar to this, but focused just on girls, for whom anaemia is a larger problem.

At the current prevalence rate, around 60 lakh adolescent girls in Rajasthan are suffering from anaemia, of which 1.2 lakh are suffering from severe anaemia.

The intervention is expected to reduce prevalence of all forms of anaemia from existing 81 percent to 47 percent, a reduction of 42 percent averting 25 lakh cases of anaemia in the target group.

With a total program cost of ₹83 crores each year, benefits would be worth more than 9-times more.

This makes a strong case to take both adolescent physical and mental health seriously.

Interventions	**BCR**	**Benefit**	**Cost**
Preventing anemia among adolescent girls (annual cost)	9	₹766 crore	₹83 crore
Delaying child marriage via direct incentives (over 4 years)	3.4	₹6,728 crore	₹2,000 crore
School based behavioral screening and further mental health services for the adolescents (annual cost)	1.4	₹264 crore	₹189 crore

Total costs and benefits are discounted at 5%

Tackling Air Pollutic
by Cleaning Up Brick Manufacturi

With an average annual production of 200 billion bricks pe num, India is the second-largest producer of bricks in the w after China. Over the last 40 years, brick production ha creased more than 8 times, due to growing demand fror housing and infrastructure sectors.

Around 35 million tonnes of coal is consumed in the sect is the third largest consumer of coal in the economy after tl power, iron and steel. Brick is a major contributor to er mental pollution as it depends heavily on natural resource

The predominant technology used for brick manufacturir dia is Fixed Chimney Bull's Trench Kiln (FBTK). This a for nearly 70 percent of the total brick produced in the However, other technologies that find application includ Kilns, which produce bricks in batches where operation happening at relatively smaller scales, and are widely u peninsular region, contributing to about 25 percent o brick production.

The brick kilns in Rajasthan are located in three maj i.e. Jaipur, Hanumangarh and Sri Ganganagar. Ambie ity monitoring takes place only at Jaipur, but reports s Sri Ganganagar has the highest share of brick kilns ir

An estimated around 801 deaths have been attributed kilns in the state.

The economic and social benefit-cost assessment u economist Souvik Bhattacharjya, Fellow, Centre Efficiency and Governance, The Energy and Resou (TERI), looks at two options for cleaner kiln techn state of Rajasthan.

The two options involve improvement of existin and FCBTK to the Zig-Zag Kilns, and Vertical Sh (VSBK) technology.

Clamp kilns and/or Fixed Chimney Kilns can be converted to Improved Zig-Zag Kilns at low costs in the lowlands at the same site. This can be accomplished in less than half a year. The production capacity is the same or higher.

Benefits and costs of improved Zig-Zag Kiln technology

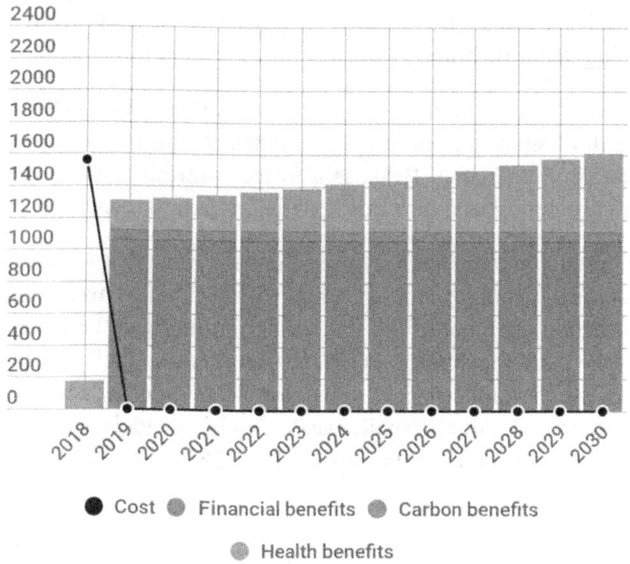

Zig-Zag brick manufacturing leads to 22 percent lower CO_2 emission than Clamp kiln/Down draught kiln brick manufacturing process. It is estimated that the cost of the proposed intervention is approx. ₹1,560 crores.

The financial benefits have been estimated for a period of 12 years (till 2030). It has been found that the production of class 1 bricks can increase from 50 percent to 80 percent in case of Zig-Zag technologies.

The total incremental financial benefits are Rs 8,911 crores till 2030. Further, with Zig-Zag technology, an estimated 362 deaths can be avoided annually (between 2019 and 2030), thereby improving quality of life.

This intervention would lead to total benefits worth ₹12,378 crores.

The VSBK technology uses hot exhaust gases for the gradual preheating of the unfired bricks in a continuous process, thus reducing energy consumption and CO2 emissions compared to the more commonly used clamp kilns.

Vertical Shaft Brik Kiln benefits and costs over time

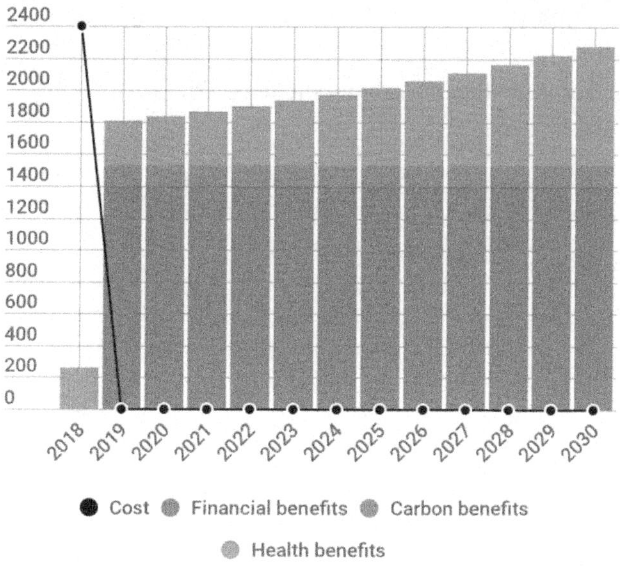

The total cost of this intervention is estimated to be approx. ₹2,400 crores.

Use of VSBK can lead to an incremental financial benefit of ₹11,760 crores. Retrofitting with VSBK technology is estimated to reduce CO2 by 2.7 million tonnes.

The avoided CO2 costs have been estimated to be Rs 1,589 crores, and an estimated 551 deaths can be avoided annually, thereby improving quality of life between 2019 and 2030. The total benefits due to conversion to VSBK technology is 17,493 crores at 5% discount rates.

This means that each intervention generates a return to society worth around 7 rupees, for every rupee spent.

Interventions	BCR	Benefit	Cost
Improved Zig-Zag kiln	8	₹12,378 crore	₹1,560 crore
Vertical Shaft Brick Kiln technologies (VSBK)	7	₹17,493 crore	₹2,400 crore

Total costs and benefits are discounted at 5%

Agriculture and Water Resource Management: How to Boost Rajasthan Farming

About 65 per cent population of Rajasthan is dependent on agriculture and allied activities for their livelihood. There exists a large variation in food grain production across states, and very high risks are involved in food grain production in the state of Rajasthan. Reducing instability in agricultural production has been a major policy concern for several years.

Two papers examine the best policies for Rajasthan to pursue to reduce water scarcity and to improve agricultural performance.

One is by Dr Dinesh Kumar, Executive Director of the Institute for Resource Analysis and Policy (IRAP), Hyderabad, and examines policies to cut water scarcity in Rajasthan.

Rajasthan is characterized by low to very low rainfall and excessively high aridity due to high temperatures affecting large parts of the state. The arid region of Western Rajasthan has vast amounts of arable land, probably the highest in India in per capita terms. The very low rainfall with high inter-annual variability and extreme aridity increase the demand for water for crop production.

The first solution examined is expansion of irrigation in the desert region of western Rajasthan through lifting canal water into "diggies" and using it for irrigation through sprinkler system and selection of crops that are less water-intensive. This enables farmers to take up crop production even in undulating land, having saline groundwater, thereby reducing irrigation water application requirements.

The annualised Capital Cost with the initial capital investment amortized is ₹16,747 per hectare.

The incremental extra income with sprinklers per hectare of irrigated crop is ₹33,900. This brings about a positive externality from water saving of 816 m3 per ha, of ₹14,986. The total benefits are worth ₹48,886 to society, meaning that each rupee spent generates nearly three rupees of benefits.

Sprinkler system irrigation annual costs and benefits per ha

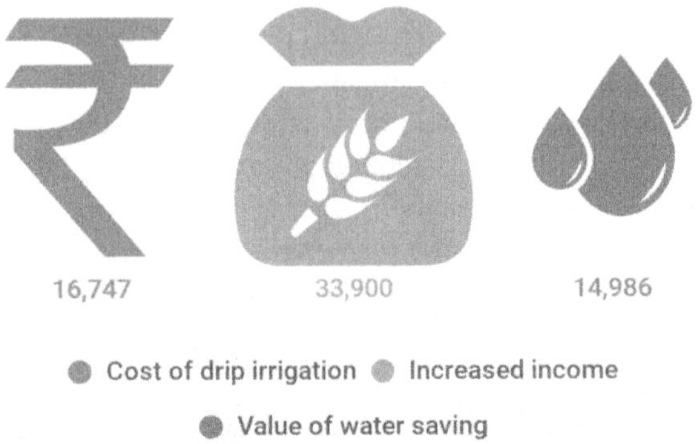

Dr Kumar also examines renovation of traditional water harvesting systems, which involves renovating Khadins for runoff harvesting for crop production in the non-rainy season. This would generate returns slightly less than the first option, but each rupee spent would still generate more than 2.5 rupees of benefits.

These are respectable returns.

But research by agricultural economist Dr. Surabhi Mittal, Independent Consultant and Non-Resident Fellow, Tata-Cornell Institute for Agriculture & Nutrition (TCI), Technical Assistance and Research for India Nutrition & Agriculture (TARINA), suggests another approach may help farmers a lot more.

This is an area where Rajasthan is already focusing. With the objective of doubling of farmer incomes, the Government of Rajasthan is focusing on increasing the seed replacement rate, enhancing crop productivity through improved soil health, crop diversification towards high value commodities, and strengthening the extension system, along with improved livestock-based systems.

The researcher looks at various methods of improving farm productivity and farmer income, including improving farm mechanization through custom hiring services; improving extension services through the use of modern ICT tools; focusing on improving soil health; and improving the availability of certified seeds.

Social and economic payback on agricultural interventions

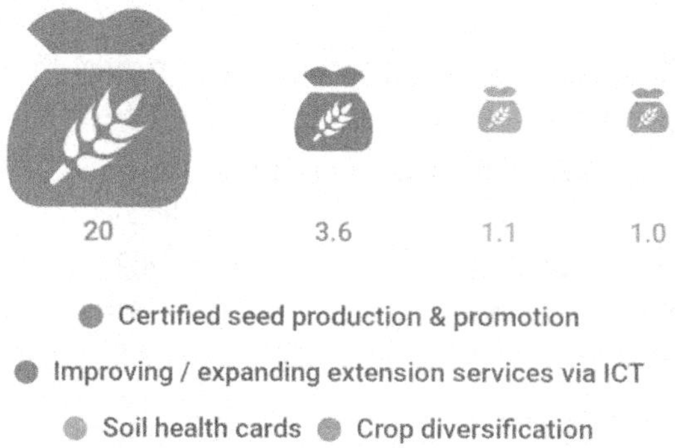

In India, farm-saved seed from previous crops remains the most prominent source of seed, year after year, accounting for nearly three-quarters of all seed usage. This means low crop productivity as optimal yield potential is a function of quality of seeds used.

Although a lot of improved varieties of seeds have been released for cultivation, their full impact has not been realized because of poor adoption rates and poor seed replacement rates.

The solution involves spending money on producing more quality seeds (for all the major crops in each state) and promoting this to farmers. The price-tag adds up to around ₹584 crores.

This will lead to better crop yields, increased production, and higher incomes. After reviewing the best evidence, the researcher suggests yield gains of ten percent can reasonably be expected with improved seed replacement rates. Even with this highly conservative assumption, the investment has huge payoffs: each rupee spent will have benefits to Rajasthan worth around 20-times the costs.

These are phenomenal benefits and highlight the need to prioritize policies that will achieve the most for farmers.

Interventions	BCR	Benefit	Cost
Certified seed production and promotion	20	₹11,586 crore	₹584 crore
Improving/expanding extension services via mobile phones	3.6	₹6,862 crore	₹1,899 crore
Expansion of efficient irrigation	2.9	₹48,886 /ha/year	₹16,747 /ha/year
Renovation of Khadins (Time horizon 15 years)	2.7	₹19,74,785 /khadin	₹7,35,875 /khadin
Soil health cards	1.1	₹2,600 crore	₹2,406 crore
Crop diversification	1.0	₹4,176 crore	₹4,074 crore

Total costs and benefits are discounted at 5%

Child Marriage: Tackling the Problem and Reducing the Insidious Impacts

While all agree that child marriage should be abolished, it continues, including in Rajasthan. As per latest National Family Health Survey (NFHS-4 2015/16), while child marriage overall has declined substantially over the last ten years, an average of 26.8% of women between the ages of 20-24 were still married before age 18 (relative to 47.4% a decade earlier). In Rajasthan, the percentage of child marriages fell from 65.2% to 35.4% over this period, but it still remains in the bottom quartile of states across India.

This has many insidious impacts. Girls that marry early typically stop going to school, meaning they receive less education, and are at a higher risk of domestic violence. In turn, their children receive less education. Child brides are much more likely to die in childbirth, and have worse health and nutrition, problems which are passed on to the next generation, who are more likely to be poor and unhealthy.

But how does Rajasthan tackle child marriage? Clearly, outlawing the practice is not sufficient. We need to find targeted policies that will help a lot while remaining cost-effective. That is the goal of Reena V. Mithal, PhD, Managing Partner of Sankhya Capital.

Experience shows that the most effective policy interventions to reduce child marriage are based on the economic empowerment of girls through secondary education.

Dr. Mithal examines four different policies that will reduce child marriage by boosting attendance at school for longer.

A typical barrier to girls' schooling is a lack of transport. Secondary school is often much further away than primary school. Without transport, more girls will stay at home, and will marry early.

Giving each girl starting in secondary school a bicycle may seem like an odd way to reduce child marriage, but it has been tested and found effective in Muralidharan and Prakash.

Over 4 years, the cost is 3316 rupees for each 14 year-old girl. About one-third of this is the cost of the bicycle, and the rest is basically the cost of the increased number of girls in school.

The policy will mean higher wages when girls graduate, because they will be better educated. Each year it will also mean fewer girls child brides which has benefits for the girls, their children, and society. (The bicycle will even save transport costs, by itself almost worth the cost of the bicycle.)

Benefits of bicycle transfers to all eligible school girls age 14

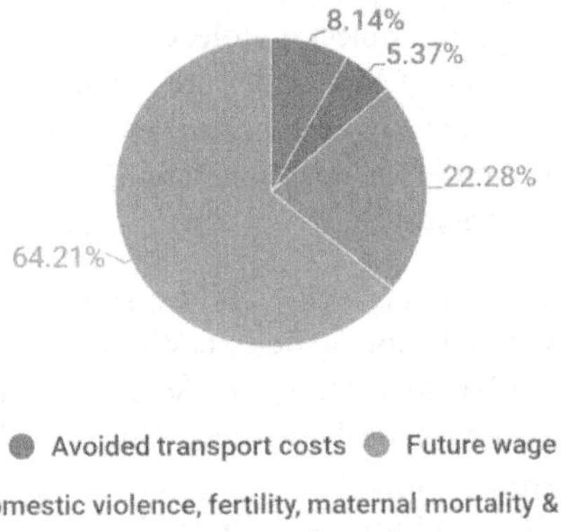

When all of these costs and benefits are compared, Dr. Mithal finds that each rupee spent will generate ₹4.50 in benefits to society, with three-quarters of the benefits coming from the increase in girls' future wages

A lack of appropriate sanitation facilities also makes girls more likely to drop out. Solving the problem means building new toilets, separating boy's and girl's toilets, and repairing toilets that need it. Those costs plus maintenance add up to a total cost of 1138 crores over 20 years. Research shows the construction of a girls-only toilet increases upper primary school enrolment by

11%, increasing future wages, and reducing child marriage and all its attendant problems. In total, each rupee will generate 4.10 rupees of social good.

Dr. Mithal also looks at the policy of using transfers to pay girls to attend school. This works well, but because it requires payments to everyone all the way through school, it is somewhat less effective, with a return to society of under three rupees for every rupee spent.

This new economic data provides new inputs for decision-makers, by highlighting the returns that can come from investment in girls' empowerment.

Interventions	BCR	Benefit	Cost
Bicycle transfer for girls' secondary school enrolment (per cohort)	4.5	₹1,645 crore	₹365 crore
Toilet provision for girls' secondary school enrolment (over 20 years)	4.1	₹4,688 crore	₹1,138 crore
Expand skill training for women (10 Lakhs young women)	4.8	₹3,263 crore	₹677 crore
Cash transfer for girls' secondary school enrolment (per cohort)	2.8	₹2,695 crore	₹951 crore

Total costs and benefits are discounted at 5%

DIGITAL INCLUSION: PREPARING FOR THE FUTURE

Digital inclusion has been the priority of Government of India and in pursuance of the same various efforts have been taken by the Government's ambitious Digital India programme like BharatNet Digi Locker, eSign Framework, National Scholarship Portal e-Hospital, and more.

Digital inclusion has been the priority of the Government of India, with various efforts taken through the ambitious Digital India programme, including BharatNet Digi Locker, eSign Framework, National Scholarship Portal e-Hospital, and more.

The National Optical Fibre Network (NOFN) is an important component of Digital India. A fully operational NOFN has the potential of bringing significant changes to the lives of rural citizens.

National Optical Fibre Network (NOFN), an ambitious initiative to trigger broadband revolution in rural India, is creating a robust middle network infrastructure layer to connect gram panchayats of the country through broadband connectivity. NOFN has been planned with an investment of ₹21,000 crore to connect 2,50,000-gram panchayats with a speed of 100 Mbps. It was established to enable key services like e-governance, education, health, banking and agriculture in rural regions of the country.

There are several challenges in the deployment of NOFN, including a lack of accountability and delays in decision-making because of an emphasis on cost controls, resulting in poor implementation. There have been delays and increases in expenditure, unavailability of affordable devices, lack of available content, and limited affordability.

Ritu Srivastava & Eshita Mukherjee of Digital Empowerment Foundation examine two options to build on India's digital inclusivity. The first of these is connecting the last sections of unconnected households via NOFN.

Currently, 8155 Gram Panchayats (GPs) in Rajasthan are connected to NOFN via 23,912 kms of optic fibre. There are around 1745 GPs which are yet not connected with NOFN.

NOFN program has been under the scanner due to delays in timeline and the quality of its services. Various telecom analysts and social scientists have criticized the program and suggested their recommendations to improve the program.

The cost is ₹7,780 crores, which includes: 1) cost of connecting the remaining GPs and ongoing maintenance; 2) cost to connect remaining households and ongoing maintenance; 3) upgrading the data centre cost to connect institutions (such as public health centre (PHC), schools, government agencies, etc) and 4) costs of accessing broadband services.

Cost over time to finalise the NOFN in crore rupees

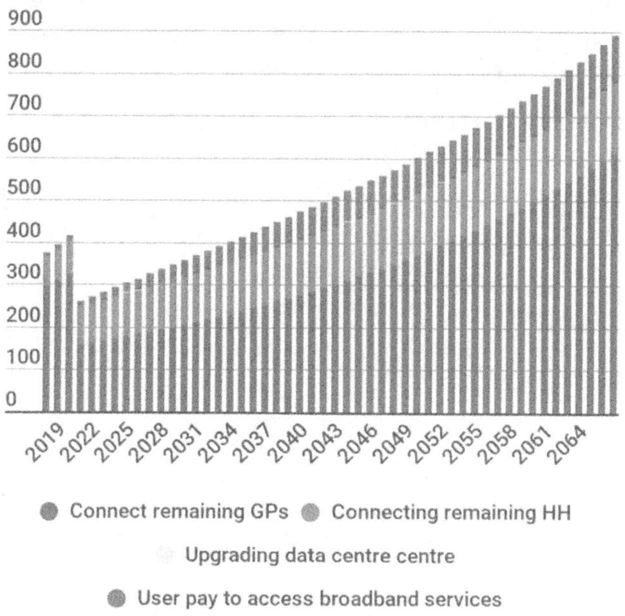

It is estimated that due to this intervention broadband would reach 17% of rural households by 2035, and 33% by 2067. Due to the falling share of rural population in the state, this will contribute to a state-wide increase in penetration of 22 per 100 households.

The World Bank estimates that 10 percent increase in broadband penetration will lead to 1.38 percent increase in GDP growth on average for low/middle income countries. It is estimated that estimate there would be annual boosts to GSDP arising from the pathway of fixed broadband growth across the entire state attributable to the NOFN. After three years the boost to GSDP is 0.02%. By 2035 the boost is 0.1%, by 2050 the boost is 0.2%, and by 2067 it is 0.3%. Total benefits until 2067 equal 69,707 crores at a 5% discount rate.

The second option focuses on the Mahatma Gandhi National Rural Employment Guarantee Act (MGNREGA). MGNREGA promises to provide 100 days of wage employment to at least one member of the estimated 150 million rural households across India. However, there have been various implementation and service delivery issues since its inception.

MGNREGA workers and Aadhaar

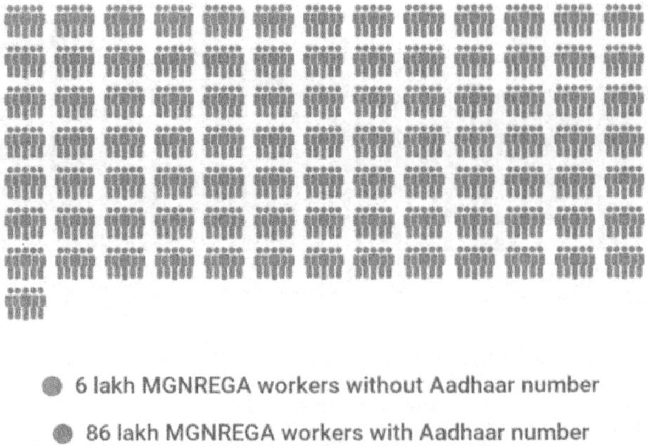

The intervention proposes transition from cash payment of MGNREGA wages to payment to the beneficiaries' bank/post office account linked to Aadhaar.

Rajasthan has been one of the top performers in implementing MGNREGA among the larger states in terms of total number of active workers (92.55 lakh as against an all-India average of 31.84 lakh in 2017–18) and also have an above-average participation rate of women (53.91 lakh as against 15.67 lakh for India in 2017–18).

Currently, there are 92 lakh active workers employed under MGNREGA and 86 lakh of them have Aadhaar numbers. Thus, the total numbers of workers to be enrolled in Aadhaar are 6 lakh. According to official statistics, all of the 86 lakh active workers with Aadhaar have enabled DBT, resulting in direct credit of wages to their Aadhaar-linked bank or post office accounts.

Although 93 percent of all active MGNREGA beneficiaries have Aadhaar numbers and receive payments in their respective bank accounts, the remaining beneficiaries need to be allotted an Aadhaar number and have their accounts linked to the DBT scheme.

This intervention targets the last seven percent of the population who are not linked to Aadhaar and DBT for year 2017-18. A multi-year projection model is built on the basis of recurring benefits for the next 15 years.

There are three categories of costs associated with this intervention. The first is bringing the remaining one percent of workers or approximately one lakh beneficiaries, under the Aadhaar scheme. The second component of costs is linking new Aadhaar account-holders to DBT, so they receive payments directly in their bank accounts. Further there is a recurring cost towards procuring biometric devices, its maintenance and connectivity etc. The total cost of the intervention is ₹24 crores over a period of 15 years.

The primary benefit of this intervention will be in reduced leakages caused by the incidences of ghost beneficiaries and deception. The benefit works out to be about six rupees for every rupee invested.

Interventions	BCR	Benefit	Cost
Providing the NOFN wired connectivity from gram panchayat (GP) to household (HH)	10	₹81,552 crore	₹7,780 crore
Linking the last section of the unconnected MGNREGA population to Aadhaar	6	₹150 crore	₹24 crore

Total costs and benefits are discounted at 5%

Early Childhood: When Education Makes the Biggest Difference

Early childhood programs have long been shown to create improvements that last a lifetime. Whether by instilling good habits or by encouraging a passion for learning, early exposure to learning cuts drop-out rates in later schooling, and generates measurable improvements to the productivity and income of adults.

The Integrated Child Development Scheme, initiated in 1975 on a pilot basis, has now grown to include 1.3 million Anganwadi centres across the country – one of the largest initiatives of its kind in the world for children under the age of six.

But the big challenge for India is to expand pre-school education access to even more children, and – crucially – to lift the quality of education offered.

Most Anganwadis operate primarily as nutrition or day-care centres with no staff formally trained in child development. Only half have basic tools for learning, like appropriate books, drawing materials, and puzzles, the government found in 2011. More than three-fifths of staff receive no help from supervisors to plan or execute educational activities, according to one recent study.

Abusaleh Shariff, Chief Scholar of the US India Policy Institute and Amit Sharma, Consultant with the World Bank in New Delhi and People Research on India's Consumer Economy, conclude that there would be significant benefits from focused investment in early childhood education.

First, they analyse the effectiveness of cash incentives to expand access further. Cash vouchers have lifted pre-school attendance in rural China. Using a similar incentive structure in Rajasthan, the total cost would run to about ₹208 crores for all 4-year olds enrolled in AWCs.

Such an incentive will likely result in a 35% increase in pre-school enrolment, taking enrolment to 29% in the short-term.

This will lead to an addition of 1.2 lakh new 4-year-olds to the state's Anganwadi preschool education program.

Cash incentive vs. lifetime wage benefit from pre-school

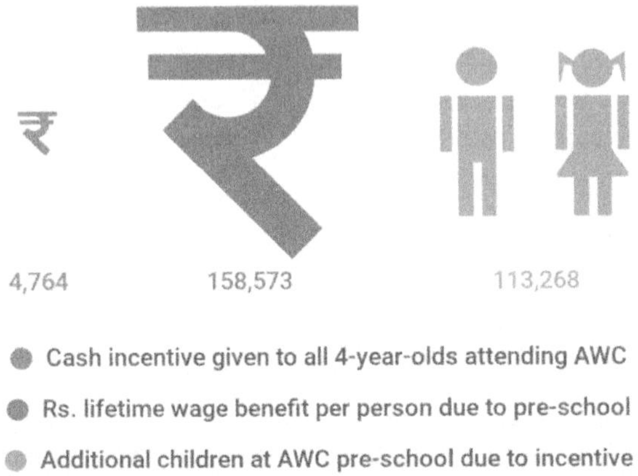

Early learning can help increase later academic achievement, build a desire to learn and aid better social and emotional development. Perhaps the most well-established result is that access to preschool education translates into an increase in future wages. Even using a conservative approach of only identifying how much more children will earn given a year of pre-school education than those who remain illiterate means an average wage increase of 23% when children grow up. For each child helped, that means more than two lakh rupees over a lifetime, or ₹1,796 crore for all of Rajasthan. In all, every rupee spent would generate benefits worth 10 rupees to society.

This approach would expand access. But how can India lift the quality of preschool education in Anganwadis? The authors look at a model already being used successfully in Karnataka, which sees spending of about ₹7,000 per year on each child aged 3-6 years enrolled in Anganwadis, on improving the quality of preschool education.

This would be enough to hire one teacher per centre, improve the curriculum, train existing Anganwadi staff, and provide uniforms and books for students. One teacher would come to the centre every day for one year.

The effect of this intervention is based on the demonstrated effectiveness from private school preschool programs. While private preschools are not perfect, they are generally regarded as providing a more appropriate environment and curriculum for children than Anganwadis.

Bringing the quality of preschool education provided through Anganwadis to a level with private preschools would cost about ₹7,200 crore per year for all the 3-6 year-olds currently enrolled at Anganwadis in Rajasthan.

The researchers' analysis concludes that this would lead to a 10% increase in average wages for the children when they grow up. With a cost of ₹776 crores, that means each rupee spent on higher quality early education generates a very generous return of ₹13.

Investment in expanding early childhood education access and improving quality would transform lives for many years to come.

Interventions	BCR	Benefit	Cost
Improving quality of PSE by partnering with localized organizations	10	₹21,815 crore	₹1,183 crore
Conditional payments for 4- year-olds to attend PSE classes at AWCs	10	₹3,479 crore	₹333 crore

Total costs and benefits are discounted at 5%

EDUCATION POLICIES TO HELP RAJASTHAN ACHIEVE ITS FULL POTENTIAL

To achieve its full potential, it is crucial that India enacts education reforms to enhance human capital. Government policies have so far lifted school enrolment and retention rates.

While more children are staying in school for longer, Pratham reports show challenges with learning outcomes: in 2005, 49 percent of Grade 5 students could do division; by 2016, it was 26 percent. Only half of children in Grade 5 can read a Grade 2 textbook.

Dr Rajesh Chakrabarti and Kushal Sagar Prakash of Sunay Policy Advisory have examined the efficiency of various education policies.

First, they look at two interventions consistent with the Right to Education Act: in-service teacher training, and reducing pupil-teacher ratios.

The authors find that even lengthy, in-depth tertiary courses and pre-service training of teachers have been found to have zero to modest effects on student learning outcomes, so it seems very unlikely that in-service training, which only occurs for a few days each year, would achieve any more.

Training costs just ₹574 per Rajasthan student annually – but the researchers conclude the policy is unlikely to generate benefits in student outcomes that are worth more to society than the cost.

Likewise, a simple analysis finds that halving the pupil-teacher ratio in Rajasthan is expensive compared to other approaches, costing ₹17,368 per student, generating benefits to learning outcomes that, in an optimistic scenario, are worth five-times the costs.

The researchers also examine ideas that are not yet official government policy but have been tested across India.

The first of these is providing performance-based incentives to teachers: effectively, paying teachers more when learning outcomes improve the most. A trial in Andhra Pradesh cost ₹552 per student per year, and resulted in better student test scores, with no evidence of any adverse consequences.

Test-score gains are linked to higher productivity in adulthood, and the researchers calculate the net effect as a 7.3 percent boost to students' wages. These concrete benefits to society are worth 24-times more than the costs of the intervention.

Next, the study examines 'teaching at the right level', which does away with grade-level curriculum and involves organising children into groups based on their current learning levels.

Lifetime values of teaching at the right level

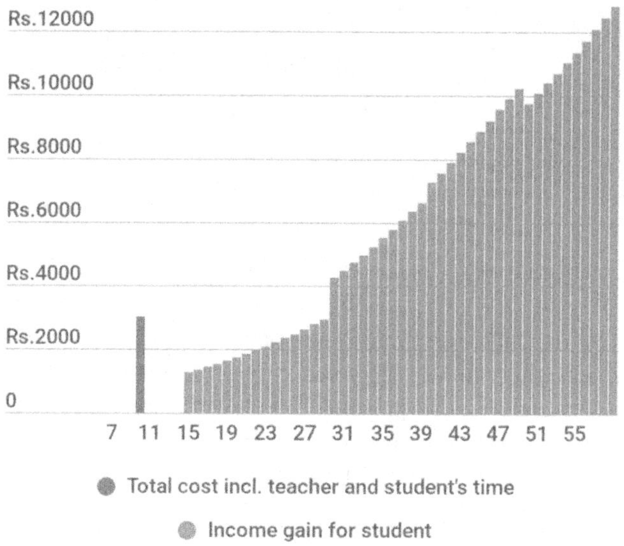

Pioneered by Pratham in India, it is deployed in two ways. The first approach involves running intensive camps, usually 80-100 hours long, with trained Pratham staff and community volunteers. The second approach involves partnership with government to embed the intervention at scale across one or more districts. Teaching at the right level can be done either outside or within existing school time.

Depending on which approach is used, the intervention generates lifelong benefits to students' incomes worth at least 19-times the costs, and up to 51-times the costs in the right conditions.

Value of future wage increase vs. cost per student in ₹

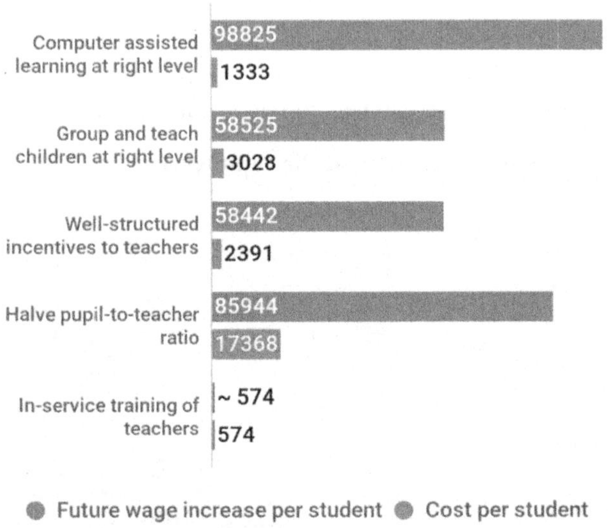

Finally, the authors examine computer-assisted learning, which uses technology to help students learn at their own level. Mindspark is one such personalised technology intervention, implemented in a rigorously measured program over five months in three low-income schools in Delhi.

Adapting this program for fifty schools, and including infrastructure, hardware, staffing and software development, would cost about ₹1333 per student over five months.

Several studies into Mindspark have shown improvements in student test-scores, and have revealed that there may be large returns to further innovation and research on effective ways of integrating technology-aided instruction into classrooms

After five months of access to the program, one robust study showed students scoring 14% higher in mathematics and 9% higher in Hindi relative to the students who didn't have access to Mindspark.

Plenty of research shows future wages are positively influenced by higher test scores. Spending just ₹1,333 per student would generate benefits to society worth ₹98,825 per student – that means that every rupee achieves 62 rupees worth of benefits.

It is policies like these that should be considered across India, to fully reap the demographic dividend. Getting children into classrooms is no longer enough. Investment in low-cost, high-impact education that will make students more productive is vital.

Interventions	BCR	Benefit	Cost
Computer assisted learning	74	₹98,825 /student	₹1,333 /student
Teaching at the right level without an extra hour	51	₹58,525 /student	₹1,157 /student
Teaching at the right level with an extra hour	19	₹58,525 /student	₹3,028 /student
Performance based incentives to teachers	24	₹58,442 /student	₹2,391 /student
50 percent reduction of pupil teacher ratio	5	₹85,944 /student	₹17,368 /student
In-service training of teachers	~1	~ ₹574 /student	₹574 /student

Total costs and benefits are discounted at 5%

Reducing Electricity Sector Losses to Power Rajasthan's Future

Inadequate and poor quality power supply means frequent interruptions, poor voltage levels, and dissatisfied consumers across much of the country.

Adding up all the losses in the system – including the losses due to energy dissipated in conductors, transformers and other equipment, along with pilferage by those who bypass meters, and losses from failure to recover the amount billed to consumers – India's total energy losses came to 24 percent in 2015-16, significantly more than international norms.

This, however, is an improvement on 2003-04 when the same losses were 38 percent. Progress was made because of national and state level reforms.

Dr Gaurav Bhatiani, Chief Operating Officer, IL&FS and his colleagues Bhawna Tyagi, and Sonali Chowdhry look at state-level solutions.

They zeroed in on the agriculture sector, one of the most inefficient electricity users. In the 1960s, the rural electrification programme was introduced to enhance agricultural output using groundwater for irrigation.

Due to un-metered supply and the flat rate electricity tariff provided for irrigation, the number of pumpsets increased substantially – and unregulated and free water has contributed to over-exploitation of groundwater resources. Subsidised power intended to benefit farmers allowed problems such as pilferage and theft, and disguised losses from the utilities, which degraded their finances.

The ultimate burden of losses is on the State Governments which collectively spent ₹36,758 crore in FY 14, ₹45,584 crore in FY15 and ₹55,283 in FY 16 (annual growth of 23%) on subsidising utilities for supplying low cost electricity for irrigation.

Distribution losses in Rajasthan at 28 percent were higher than the national average of 24 percent in FY16.

Nationally, one of the major reasons for the high losses was the adoption of a low-tension distribution network spread over long distances to serve dispersed, small, individual agriculture connections. This resulted not only in high technical losses, but also in theft facilitated by unmetered supply and the flat tariff.

The degradation of the utilities' finances has adversely affected farmers by making the supply and quality of power unpredictable and by providing it mainly during the night hours. This resulted in frequent failure of pumpsets, forcing farmers to use inefficient motors , and keep the pumpsets constantly on, wasting energy and overexploitation of groundwater.

All in all, this is a vicious cycle in which farmers, distribution companies, and State Governments alike all face ever-increasing losses.

The researchers propose two solutions. The first is to introduce a high-voltage distribution system (HVDS), by upgrading the network and replacing transformers.

Implementation of HVDS will improve voltage profile, reduce LT Line losses, and lower the chances of failure of distribution transformer and pumpset burn-out.

Completing the upgrade would cost ₹19,655 crore. The biggest saving would come from the fact that pumpsets wouldn't fail so often. Factoring in carbon savings, energy savings, and the reduction in transformer failure, the total benefits would come to ₹43,350.

In short, each rupee invested would generate a return worth more than two rupees.

The second solution proposed by the researchers, replacing inefficient pumpsets with energy efficient ones, further enhances the return on investment. s

The total costs would larger, because we would need not only the high-voltage distribution system to be set up, but also replace all existing pumps: a total bill of ₹26,386 crore. Yet, the total benefits would also grow, allowing each rupee to generate more than three rupees of social benefits, both through lower pump breakage, along with energy savings and carbon savings.

Crore ₹ costs and benefits of agricultural power upgrade to high-voltage and installing energy efficient water pumps

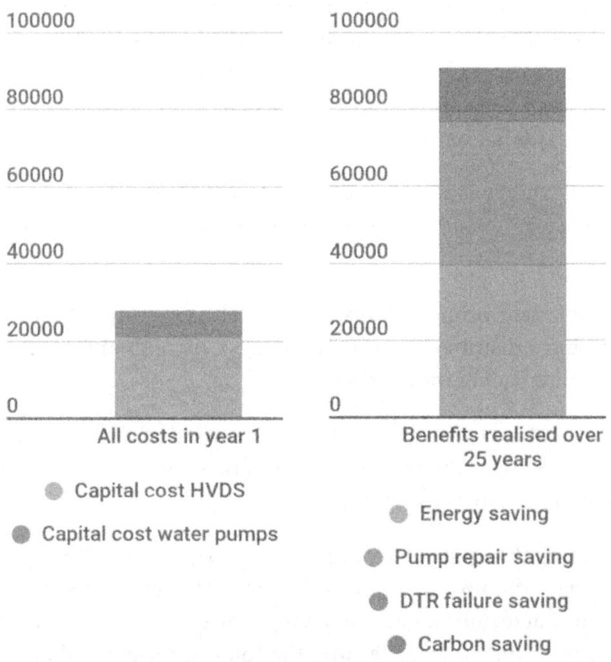

Both these interventions will also result in a significant indirect benefit by enabling reduction in the subsidy by Governments for irrigation, which can be redirected to other areas.

Anandajit Goswami of the TERI School of Advanced Studies, and Kaushik Ranjan Bandyopadhyay of the Indian Institute of Management examine rising energy demand in buildings, which is accompanied by a rise in electricity use leading to a rapid increase in carbon emissions and aggravating power shortages. They show the benefits of using water- or salt-based thermal energy storage in buildings, and find the investment would have a return worth more than two rupees for every rupee spent in Rajasthan.

This highlights both the lasting challenges that can be caused by well-meaning policy decisions such as the low-tension distribution network and introducing energy efficient pumpsets but also the opportunities that exist to reduce losses in the power sector. This would be a win-win for everyone.

Gaurav Bhatiani, Chief Operating Officer of IL&FS, and Harsha Meenawat, Assistant Manager of IL&FS study "last mile electrification". As of October 2017, 10 districts in Rajasthan reported less than 50% achievement in household electrification. Of these, Bikaner district was selected for study as it reported a relatively low 49% achievement on the intensive electrification (households) program and only 16% Below Poverty Line (BPL) households with access to electricity. Further, 62% of rural households in Bikaner, Rajasthan have been electrified and the balance 38% do not have access as per Saubhagya scheme online dashboard.

Social, economic and environmental return on investment of electricity access to unserved population

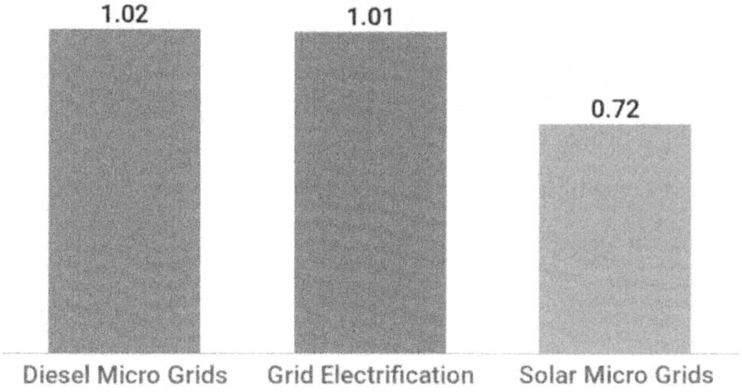

Using solar micro grids would be the most expensive approach, with a cost of 11,350 crore, generating a return that is less than one rupee for each rupee spent.

Diesel micro grids and grid electrification both fare better, with returns worth more than one rupee.

These studies highlight the range of options for policy-makers in Rajasthan to consider when trying to ensure that the benefits of electricity reach everyone.

Interventions	BCR	Benefit	Cost
HVDS and EEPS - Upgrade agricultural power distribution to high voltage and energy efficient agricultural water pumps	3.4	₹90,780 crore	₹26,386 crore
HVDS - Upgrade agricultural power distribution to high voltage	2.3	₹45,350 crore	₹19,655 crore
Water based thermal energy storage for commercial buildings	2.7	₹1,448 /sq. ft.	₹531 /sq. ft.
Salt hybrid based thermal energy storage for commercial buildings	2.6	₹1,448 /sq. ft.	₹566 /sq. ft.
Diesel micro grids for 'last mile electrification'	1.0	₹2,784 crore	₹2,722 crore
Grid electrification for 'last mile electrification'	1.0	₹2,736 crore	₹2,717 crore
Solar micro grids for 'last mile electrification'	0.7	₹8,126 crore	₹11,350 crore

Total costs and benefits are discounted at 5%

THE REAL STRATEGIES TO REDUCE FARMER DISTRESS

In Rajasthan, promising policies could help to reduce farmer distress. Professor Nilanjan Banik from Bennett University, Greater Noida studied responses to farmer distress. This is generally less of a problem in Rajasthan than elsewhere. Among all the states in India, Rajasthan has one of the lowest farmer suicide rates. Between 2010 and 2012, there were 3.6 farmer suicides per 1000 population. The corresponding figure for all India during the same period was 15 per 1000 population. In terms of land-holding size, small and marginal farmers in the state constitute 58.4% share of the total area. Big farmers - with farm size more than 10 ha - hold 33.3% of the total area.

In February 2018, Rajasthan Government announced one-time loan waiver of up to ₹50,000 for small (between 1 and 2 ha land size) and marginal farmers (with less than 1 ha land size) in the state. This is estimated to cost ₹8000 crores to the state exchequer. Last year, Uttar Pradesh, Maharashtra and Punjab undertook large-scale farm debt waivers, costing half a percent of the entire GDP of India, and Andhra Pradesh has recently announced a loan waiver costing ₹ 24,000 crore.

However, the research by Professor Banik, supported by other economic studies, finds that a loan waiver scheme costs about as much as it achieves. Moreover, it mostly helps richer and bigger farmers, leaving smaller farmers worse off in the future.

Only 15% of the marginal farmers (with less than 1 hectare of landholding) have access to formal credit, so a loan waiver helps them little, and previous waivers have led to banks reducing credit for small farmers.

Professor Banik's analysis for Rajasthan shows that waiving formal loans for land holders with less than two hectares would cost ₹11,731 crores. The benefits will be slightly lower at ₹9,537 crores. This also means a 15% reduction in smallholder credit over the following years, cutting revenue for the most vulnerable farmers by 13.5%. And spending thousands of crores on less effective policy leaves less for much more effective ones.

Total formal credit held by farmers

But other interventions could be much more helpful.

What interventions, then, could be more helpful? One answer is reducing waste of perishable fruits, vegetables and milk that command a higher market price than staple crops. Most small farmers do not risk growing perishable crops. Nearly 20% of India's fresh produce is wasted because of storage problems.

The National Centre for Cold Chain Development (NCCD) has estimated Rajasthan's total requirement for storing milk, fruits and vegetables at 74,889 metric tonnes. Providing pack houses and trucks would cost ₹5,985 crores. The benefits in terms of the reduced wastage in milk, fruits and vegetables, are worth more than 15-times that figure.

And, in Rajasthan, the largest producer of coarse grains, Professor Banik's research suggests that e-markets could result in better prices. Rajasthan has 114 agricultural markets that are yet to be "e-enabled". Factoring in the one-time total, fixed cost of introducing e-mandi, and operational costs increasing over time, the annualised cost of setting up and running e-mandis over 20 years is ₹131 crores. Farmers would realize better prices with reduced information asymmetry and direct market access, meaning a 13% price increase - basically a transfer from middlemen to farmers. The research suggests that in Rajasthan, farmers would gain ₹8,523 crore over 20 years. Benefits are an astonishing 65-times the costs. This makes it an incredibly powerful policy for Rajasthan.

Farmer distress requires a serious response – but as in everything, there are choices. Economic analysis clearly shows that each rupee could achieve vast benefits – or could do as little as 80 paise. It is important to follow the evidence.

Interventions	BCR	Benefit	Cost
Introduction of e-mandis (Time horizon 20 years)	65	₹8,523 crore	₹131 crore
Cold chain infrastructure (Time horizon 10 years)	16	₹92,788 crore	₹5,985 crore
Farm loan waiver (Time horizon 5 years)	0.8	₹9,537 crore	₹11,731 crore

Total costs and benefits are discounted at 5%

Reducing Domestic Violence Would Have Vast Economic Benefits

Rajasthan would enjoy an economic boon worth thousands of crores of rupees if it steps up efforts to reduce domestic violence.

Globally, violence between intimate partners is huge: it costs the world 25-times more than all wars and terrorism. In India, the latest National Family Health Survey shows that 22 percent of married women aged 15-49 experienced spousal physical or sexual violence in the past 12 months. That suggests that in India, at least five crore women were assaulted last year.

Violence against women the past year

Yet, there has been relatively little research into reducing this devastating impact. Despite nearly a decade of implementation, evidence of the effectiveness of the 2005 Domestic Violence Act is fragmentary at best. The few available assessments suggest there is a lack of clarity within the judiciary about interpretation, inadequate money is allocated to establish required infrastructure, and there is too little awareness about the law among judges, protection officers and civil society, as well as among women.

It is clear that legislation alone is not enough to change outdated norms that underpin violence.

Research from Srinivas Raghavendra, Mrinal Chadha, and Nata Duvvury of the University of Ireland Galway helps close gaps in the evidence – and points to sizable economic benefits from reducing domestic violence.

The researchers study two of the very few approaches that there is empirical evidence of effectiveness.

The first is based on the SASA! project, which is a community mobilisation intervention seeking to change the norms and behaviours that result in gender inequality, violence and increased HIV vulnerability for women, pioneered in Uganda and used in more than 20 countries.

The approach, costing ₹980 per person, guides communities through a process in which people are repeatedly exposed to the programme. New attitudes and norms that promote more equitable relationships diffuse throughout the community.

The researchers suggest that this community mobilisation intervention could target women aged 15-59 years below the poverty line who have been in a partnership in the past year. In Rajasthan this would mean reaching 18 lakh women for a price-tag of ₹183 crore.

Of these 18 lakh women, more than 5 lakh would be assaulted by a spouse annually. Based on studies in India and abroad, it is likely each of these women will on average experience abuse 8-times a year.

The second intervention, used in South Africa, combines microfinance with training about domestic violence, gender norms and sexuality, thus providing women with the means and knowledge to improve their well-being.

The study explores the effects of using the intervention to target the same women over a two-year trial, followed by a two-year scale-up. It would cost about ₹850 per person, meaning a program cost of ₹159 Crores in Rajasthan.

In their original countries, both programs led to an estimated 55% reduction in domestic violence by the end of the intervention, and benefits that were estimated to last for at least another four years.

Either of these programs would avoid many medical injuries including eye injuries, bruises, dislocations, and broken bones, and even some deaths.

This has spillover effects. Women who are victims of spousal abuse have to miss paid work, unpaid domestic work, and free time. Each assault on average costs a woman 5.5 days.

This reduction in productivity is a huge loss to the Rajasthan economy. The cost to the entire formal and informal economy in 2018 from all married women is a whopping ₹8,200 crore.

Targeting 18 lakh women would help some 2 lakh women avoid abuse, leading to benefits in total worth ₹2,360 crore. Each rupee spent could still help avoid damages worth around 10 rupees.

Reducing domestic violence is not only morally imperative, but can help Rajasthan become more productive and generate benefits worth many thousands of crores of rupees.

Interventions	BCR	Benefit	Cost
Self Help Group-based Intervention for combating Violence Against Women (SHGIVAW)	11	₹1,717 crore	₹159.4 crore
Community Mobilisation-Based Intervention for Combating Violence Against Women (CMBIVAW)	9	₹1,717 crore	₹183.9 crore

Total costs and benefits are discounted at 5%

Top Healthcare Priorities for Investment

The Indian healthcare sector has improved in both quality and quantity, enhancing the wellbeing of communities and the development of the nation. This is most evident in the dramatic increase in life expectancy: In 1901, the average Indian lived just 24 years. Even after independence, in 1951 life expectancy had climbed to a paltry 32 years. Today, the average Indian reaches 69 years of life, or more than what used to be two lifetimes.

This is because of a phenomenal decline in infant and maternal deaths, because major communicable diseases have been brought under control, and smallpox and polio have been eliminated.

However, the overall performance of the healthcare sector remains below international benchmarks. When it comes to strengthening the entire system, what should be the priorities for investment?

Looking at ways to strengthen the healthcare system, the first approach recommended by researchers PR Sodani, Neeraj Sharma, Md Mahbub Hossain, SD Gupta,, and DK Mangal of IIHMR University, Jaipur, is to improve the service quality of maternal health interventions. This requires a string of investments across the entire course of human birth, from ensuring family planning for the last few who still lack access, to ensuring that all mothers are provided with transportation and access to facility births or have skilled attendants at home births. It also involves improving availability of more high-tech equipment and personnel to tackle serious complications like obstructed labour, ante-partum and post-partum haemorrhage and eclampsia.

In Rajasthan, the researchers find that ensuring all women have access to all or almost all of these interventions will over the next two decades cost about ₹11,495 crores. These interventions are estimated to result in a reduction of maternal mortality by 66%, saving 2,827 maternal lives per year. They would also reduce neonatal mortality by 20%, saving 6,542 new-born lives per year.

Put into financial terms, the total benefits to society would be worth ₹111,563 crores. In other words, each rupee spent on these maternal health interventions would generate benefits worth 9.7 rupees.

Averted deaths per year from improved maternal health care

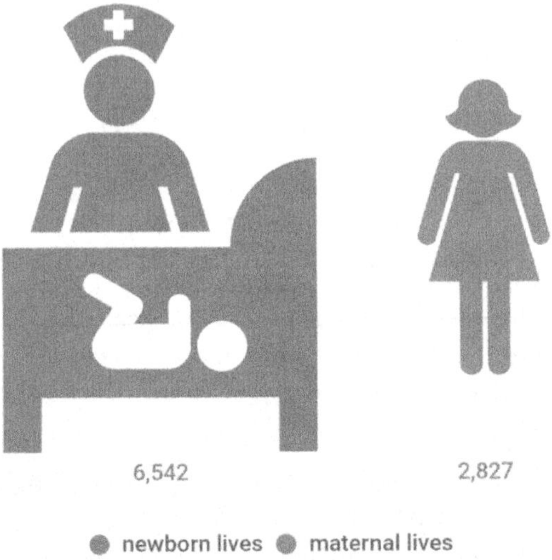

A shortage of ambulances means that people die due to delays in reaching timely healthcare facilities. Prior research suggests that generally, there should be about 33 ambulances for every million people in urban areas, and three-times more in rural areas.

The new analysis shows some tough choices need to be made. Providing sufficient ambulances for the urban areas of Rajasthan would over a decade cost about a thousand crore rupees. But it would save 3,047 lives each year among patients of Ischemic heart disease, road traffic accidents, and obstructed labour. Each rupee spent on strengthening ambulance services would generate social benefits worth a very worthy ₹8.8.

But the researchers' analysis shows that there is a huge difference in the efficiency of serving urban and rural areas. An adequate number of ambulances in rural Rajasthan could save around five-times the number of lives each year. But unfortunately, the cost would skyrocket to 12-times the cost of urban ambulances. Each rupee invested would generate more modest social benefits worth ₹3.3. These are still considerable returns compared to many policy choices, but the stark difference highlights challenging decisions that policymakers will need to make.

Improved ambulance services 10-year costs and benefits

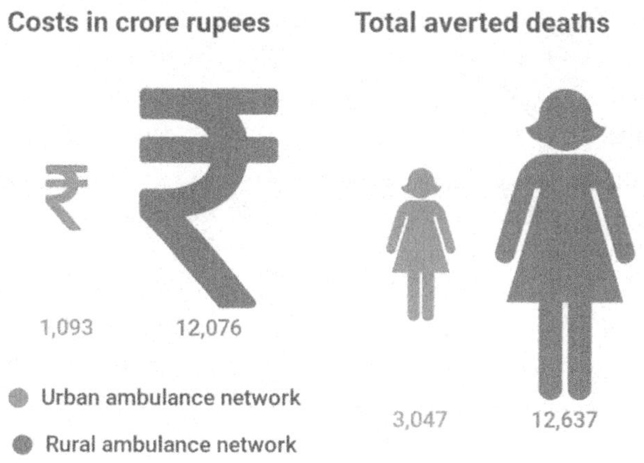

Finally, the researchers highlight the huge benefits from investment in family planning, to help women ensure space between pregnancies. Doing so has a huge range of benefits: it prevents unwanted pregnancy-related health risks in women, indirectly reduces infant mortality, reduces the spread of sexually transmitted diseases, empowers people and enhances education, reduces adolescent pregnancy, and helps in reducing population growth. Roughly five percent of the female population in the state still need contraceptives. Targeting these women is a challenge, but this can be achieved by expanding access to family planning services.

The total cost is ₹614 crores for Rajasthan. Most benefits come from demographic dividends but also from child and maternal lives saved due to family planning methods would also be important. The total economic and social benefits would be worth about ₹19,728 crore for Rajasthan. This means every rupee would generate societal benefits worth about 32-times the investment.

These quite remarkable returns highlight the impact that can be made by carefully focusing on further strengthening health systems, to close remaining gaps.

Interventions	BCR	Benefit	Cost
Family planning for unmet need (annualised)	32	₹19,728 /capita	₹614 /capita
Strengthening basic and surgical capacity for reducing maternal and neonatal deaths (Time horizon 20 years)	10	₹111,563 crore	₹11,495 crore
Improved urban 108 ambulance services (Time horizon 10 years)	9	₹9,645 crore	₹1,093 crore
Improved rural 108 ambulance services (Time horizon 10 years)	3.3	₹39,762 crore	₹12,076 crore

Total costs and benefits are discounted at 5%

Improving the Ease of Doing Business: Land Record Reform Will Open Doors for Business

While India climbed a phenomenal 30 spots to the 100th position out of 190 surveyed countries in the World Bank's 'ease of doing business' index this year, investors have ample choice among Indian states.

Investor perception is key, and each state wants to make sure that it is competitive. New research findings identify specific policies that would help gain an advantage. In the last few years, Rajasthan has emerged as a preferred destination for business, mainly due to its proximity to the national capital, and an immense pool of resources in areas such as minerals, tourism, handicrafts, renewable energy, etc. Rajasthan's contribution towards India's GDP has been, on an average, 4.8 per cent in the last 11 years. The unemployment rate of 14.3 percent as in March 2018 is the highest ever that Rajasthan has witnessed over the last two years and thus, emphasizes the need to boost private sector investment in the state. Businesses in Rajasthan continue to witness various administrative and regulatory issues on a regular basis.

Nirupama Soundararajan and Shagun Khurana from Pahle India Foundation have looked at how business reforms can help Rajasthan get ahead.

The researchers suggest that to streamline the land market further, the state government needs to move towards a conclusive land titling system. All records related to land – including record of rights, maps, and surveys – need to be digitised.

The computerization of existing land records is nearly complete in Rajasthan, with computerised copies of Record of Rights (RORs) available for a nominal fee in 97 per cent of the villages through kiosk centres established in each taluka. However, the overall physical progress in Rajasthan in other components of Digital India Land Records Modernization Programme (DILRMP) has been rather slow.

Two specific interventions to improve the land records management system in Rajasthan are proposed: (a) completion of survey/resurvey activities, and (b) digitisation of cadastral maps.

Completion of survey and re-survey activities and digitisation of cadastral maps will have a total cost of about ₹486 crores. However, this will have multiple benefits. Evidence shows that strengthening property rights reduces the risk of expropriation and corruption. It also improves the mechanisms for peaceful resolution of disputes and contract enforcement. Perhaps most importantly, as land is more securely owned, it will be more advantageous for investors to spend money making land more productive, because owners are more likely to reap the benefits. This will all drive economic growth.

Based on a raft of studies across the world showing how more secure property rights drive the economy, the researchers calculate this would mean a 0.024 percentage point boost to the growth rate of the economy of Rajasthan – which may sound slight, but would equate to ₹12598 crores, or benefits that are worth nearly 26-times the costs.

Ensuring that investors can buy and sell land with confidence is a winner.

The researchers also examine a second approach: incubation support. Incubation is a business support process aimed at successful development of start-up companies by providing entrepreneurs with an array of targeted resources and services required at the initial stage.

The total cost of this intervention is a sum of cost of construction of the incubator, cost of lease on land, cost of maintenance and operations, cost of mentoring and training, cost of equity provided by incubator to graduating start-ups. investment funding received by incubated start-ups from other investors and increase in R&D spending by the private sector.

If assuming a value addition of 3.5x due to incubation the total cost of setting up an incubation centre and working space in Jaipur, along with additional funds required for investment and

R&D is estimated at ₹9.53 crores per annum; in a scenario with 6x value addition, the total cost comes to ₹9.67 crores per annum.

The total benefit resulting from the incubation support is estimated to be around ₹15.68 crores per annum when the value addition is 3.5 times, or ₹17.68 crores per annum with 6x value assumption. In either case, the benefits are fairly slight, at between one and two rupees for every rupee spent.

Interventions	BCR	Benefit	Cost
Land record management system, conducting survey and re-survey activities, and digitise cadastral maps	26	₹12,598.30 crore	₹486.39 crore
Start-up incubator support: Scenario I (3.5x value addition)	1.7	₹111.48 crore	₹66.11 crore
Start-up incubator support: Scenario II (6x value addition)	1.9	₹136.55 crore	₹72.88 crore

Total costs and benefits are discounted at 5%

MOTHER-AND-CHILD HEALTH: A SMART OPPORTUNITY TO TRANSFORM LIVES IN RAJASTHAN

Rajasthan has improved significantly on its maternal and child survival indicators in the last 10 years. Between 2005-06 and 2015-16, Rajasthan's infant mortality fell from 65 to 41 deaths per 1000 live births. Maternal mortality rate fell from 318 per 100,000 live births in 2008, to 244 in 2013.

Nevertheless, there is still room for improvement, particularly on several indicators related to access and use of child and maternal health services. Abusaleh Shariff, Chief Scholar of the US-India Policy Institute, looks at this situation.

The first intervention Dr. Shariff suggests is providing an incentive to each mother, expanding the present-day system.

Cash incentive for ANC visits cost breakdown

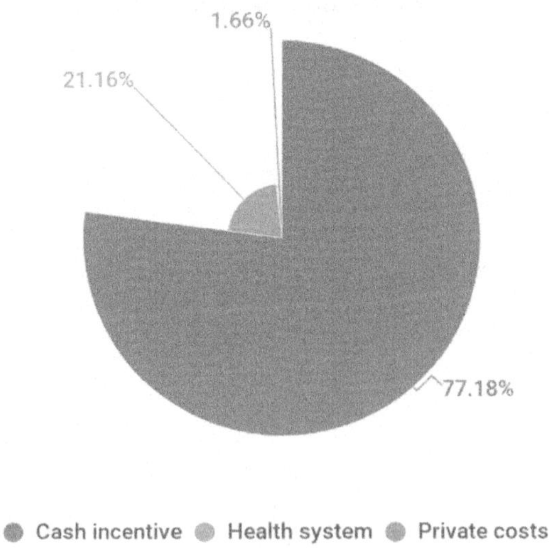

The total cost for Rajasthan is ₹241 crores, with the bulk being cash incentives. (The remainder is increased costs to the health system and private costs to mothers). It is assumed this incentive will boost uptake of 4 ANC services from 39 percent to 61 percent of women during pregnancy.

Literature review suggests that 25% reduction in neonatal deaths is a reasonable estimate of the impact in the Indian context from increased ANC visits. It is expected that this will lead to a reduction in neonatal mortality of 8 per 1000 live births. This will save 2,764 infant lives per year.

In this case, Dr. Shariff estimates the benefits are ₹2,097 crores annually. Every rupee achieves nine rupees of benefits to society, which is a good return on investment.

Promotion of breastfeeding cost breakdown

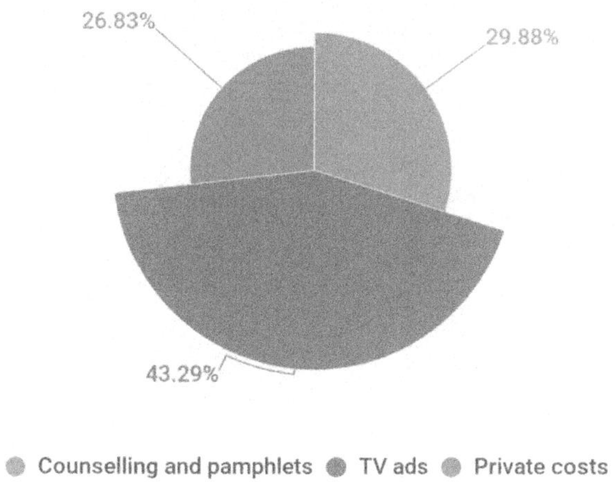

The researcher also studies a breastfeeding mass media campaign, using television advertisements and counselling. It is estimated that this intervention will increase exclusive breastfeeding from 58 percent to 90 percent, and extended breastfeeding from 75 percent to 94 percent. This implies an additional 4.8 lakh children more who will be exclusively breastfed, and 2.8 lakh who will be breastfed between 6-23 months.

The benefits are worth 8-times the costs.

By far the most compelling case in the new research paper is for expanding immunisation programs in lagging districts. In Rajasthan only 55% of the children are fully vaccinated. Further there are districts where full immunization rates are below the state average (Jalore, Barmer, Jaisalmer, Jodhpur, Chittorgarh, Udaipur, Nagaur, Banswara, Sawai Modhopur, Sirohi and Alwar). The average rate of immunization in these districts is 43%, compared to the state average of 55 percent.

Immunisation rate in lagging districts

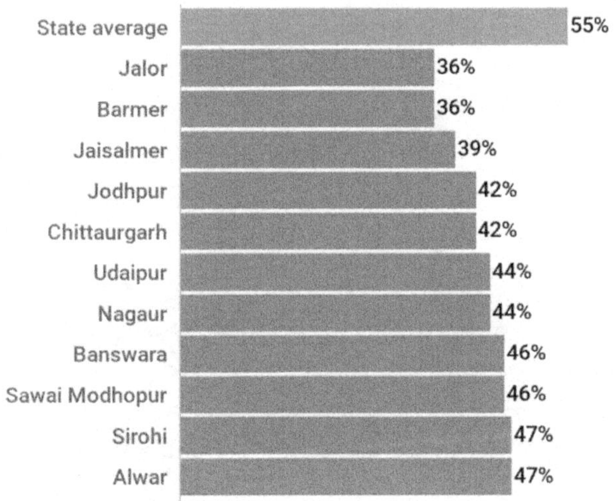

This intervention targets these districts.

Based on a trial already held successfully in Rajasthan, Dr. Shariff proposes setting up 'immunization camps' in the lagging districts, providing lentils and meals to parents for vaccinating their children. The policy would cost ₹24.2 crores in Rajasthan and, if it raised the level of fully immunized children to the state average, would save 827 children annually.

Immunization would generate benefits worth ₹30 for every rupee spent, which is a considerable return on investment.

New data on costs and benefits closes evidence gaps and helps ensure more good can be done with each rupee. Focusing on interventions to further improve mother and child health would help save lives and strongly enhance the overall wellbeing of Rajasthan.

Interventions	BCR	Benefit	Cost
Immunization promotion, incentivization and supply in lagging districts (annual)	30	₹720 crore	₹24 crore
Conditional cash transfer for ANC visits (annual)	9	₹2,097 crore	₹241 crore
Breastfeeding mass media promotion and intensive counselling (annual)	8	₹9,227 crore	₹1,181 crore

Total costs and benefits are discounted at 5%

Non-Communicable Diseases: Huge Payoffs from Focus on Diabetes and Heart Disease

India's rapid growth means infectious diseases are increasingly being vanquished. Yet, as more people live longer lives, this is somewhat counterbalanced by an increase in the toll of chronic disease – what the health community calls non-communicable diseases (NCDs). According to the Global Burden of Disease, 54% of all Indian deaths in 1990 were due to communicable diseases (along with maternal, neonatal and nutritional diseases), whereas just 38% came from NCDs (the last 8% were caused by injuries). But since 2001, NCDs have claimed more lives. By 2016 they caused 62% of all deaths. This will only keep increasing, with one estimate showing NCDs and mental health conditions will cost India an astonishing $4.58 trillion between 2012 and 2030 – about twice the total GDP of India today.

Recognizing this shift, the Government launched the National Program for Prevention and Control of Cancer, Diabetes, CVD and Stroke (NPCDCS) in 2011. Most states have initiated activities with technical and financial support from the central government. However, much more needs to be done, since there are many more lives that can be saved.

Professor Shreelata Rao Seshadri of Azim Premji University, with co-author Vijayalakshmi Hebbare, show that policy-makers can achieve a lot by prioritizing particular strategies against specific NCDs.

Take diabetes. It will cost India ₹9.7 trillion (USD$150 billion) between 2012 and 2030. Diabetes causes about 30 in every 100,000 deaths in Rajasthan, about 40% of which could be averted by early detection and treatment with Metformin. Metformin is a well-recognized cost-effective treatment for prediabetes and diabetes, resulting in avoidance of diabetes in about 30% of high risk individuals.

The solution is screening and putting people with high blood sugar will be put on a regimen of 850 mg Metformin twice a day. The target population for this intervention are people aged between 30-69 years with the aim of 50% coverage of the target group annually, and the assumption of achieving 65% adherence to treatment. The average cost per treated individual is estimated at ₹2,197 for males and ₹2,101 for females.

It is estimated that 40% of the deaths can be averted over a 13-year period with Metformin therapy. Assuming 65 % adherence to Metformin therapy about 15,150 projected diabetes deaths could be prevented in Rajasthan.

This means that every rupee achieves 16 rupees of benefits.

However, some NCDs don't present such simple solutions. The authors look at cervical cancer and breast cancer, both serious problems that need tackling. Unfortunately, screening costs are around the same level as those to tackle CVD, yet the benefits are much lower. Cervical cancer causes about 11 out of every 100,000 deaths each year in Rajasthan, but an ambitious screening and treatment program would be expensive, costing ₹4,693 crore, to save about 1,000 lives annually. The return on each rupee is just 1.4 rupees in social benefits. Breast cancer screening would be just as costly, saving hundreds of lives annually.

The evidence is very compelling for combating cardiovascular disease (CVD), which is a leading killer in India. By itself, it will cost 130 trillion rupees between 2012 and 2030 – almost the equivalent of eradicating one year of India's entire GDP.

In the age group 30-69, CVD causes 3 percent of Rajasthan's deaths. The answer is relatively simple: a screening program to identify those at high risk, and putting those with elevated blood pressure on a cheap "polypill". The target population for this intervention are people aged between 30-69 years assessed as being at high risk and those with existing cardiovascular disease. The target would be to screen 70% of this population with the assumption of achieving 60% adherence to treatment. The average cost per treated individual is estimated at ₹4,202 for males and ₹4,106 for females. In total, each rupee spent will achieve benefits worth 23 times expenditure, and save 260,000 lives between 2018 and 2030, or around 21,000 lives each year – more than all of the other investments combined.

India's development will make NCDs the next great health challenge, but not all investments are equally effective. The evidence shows that adequate coverage of screening and treatment services at the primary level for diabetes and especially for heart disease can avert a large number of deaths in a very cost-effective manner. These arguments should make such programs very attractive for politicians in Rajasthan.

Comparison of costs and averted deaths

Total costs in crore rupees over 14 years

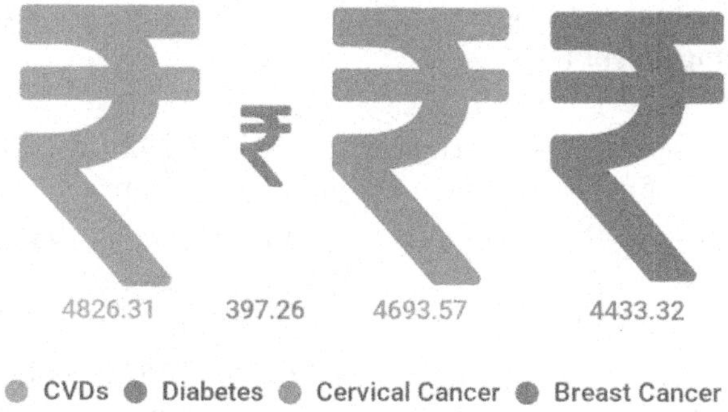

Total averted deaths

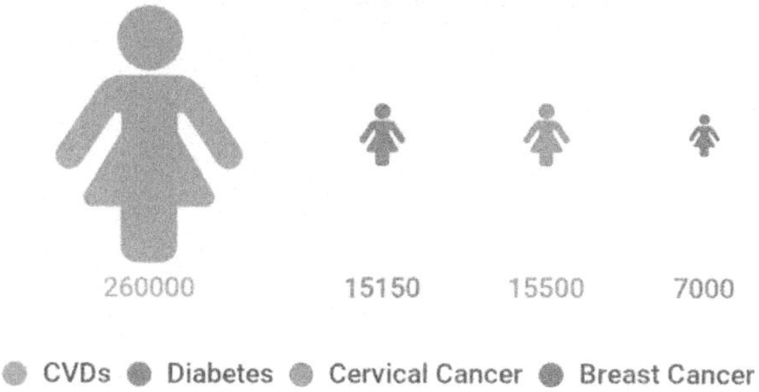

Interventions	BCR	Benefit	Cost
Secondary prevention of cardio-vascular disease through use of a multidrug polypill (total costs for 14 years)	23	₹111,886 crore	₹4,823 crore
Diabetes screening and treatment (total costs for 14 years)	16	₹6,421 crore	₹397 crore
Cervical cancer screening and treatment (total costs for 14 years)	1.4	₹6,523 crore	₹4,694 crore
Breast cancer screening and treatment (total costs for 14 years)	0.7	₹2,925 crore	₹4,433 crore

Total costs and benefits are discounted at 5%

NUTRITION: A DEVELOPMENT INVESTMENT FOR THE AGES

Proper early nutrition can spectacularly change the entire life trajectory of a child. We know from long-term studies that it promotes brain development, making the child do better in school, and much better later in life, affecting everything from the happiness of marriages to the quality of jobs, and up to 60% more earnings.

India has made significant progress in reducing child malnutrition, but with nearly half of all deaths of children aged under-five mainly caused by poor diet, much still needs to be done. Where could new policies make the biggest impact?

William Joe and Abhishek Kumar of Institute of Economic Growth, and S.V. Subramanian of Harvard T. H. Chan School of Public Health, have undertaken analysis on how Rajasthan could reach more young children and pregnant and lactating mothers.

In Rajasthan, essential health and nutrition inputs reach less than 55 percent of mothers and children and the consequences of poor nutrition manifest in terms of growth failure of child, reduced learning capacity, increased rate of morbidity and mortality.

Direct nutrition-based interventions include counselling for behaviour change, supplementary food and micronutrient supplements, which are primarily delivered through the government health programmes. A 10 percent increase in coverage would avoid 365 deaths, and reduce stunting by 20% in the population receiving the intervention. Each rupee spent will be worth 6 rupees in benefits.

The health status of a child is inextricably linked to the health status of the mother. Women who are anaemic are likely to deliver low birth weight babies, who are likely to remain anaemic and suffer from cumulative growth and development deficit. Adequate nutritional health is critical for safe motherhood and to break the otherwise perpetual intergenerational cycle of undernutrition. In India, there is very high prevalence of both maternal and child undernutrition.

Proportion of reproductive-age women anaemia

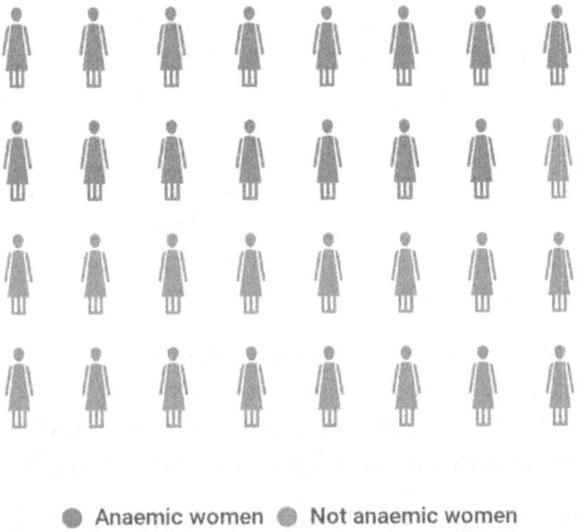

All children below 6 years of age, pregnant women and lactating mothers are eligible for availing of supplementary food services under the Integrated Child Development Scheme (ICDS) which is funded by both Central and State government. Supplementary nutrition need to be better targeted towards those sections that actually require the appropriate nutrition.

The primary beneficiaries are children aged 6-12 and 12-36 months and pregnant and lactating women. The benefits will accrue through reduction in deaths and morbidity from specific diseases due to provision of improved nutrition. It is estimated 324 lives will be saved. At a cost of 11,532 rupees per beneficiary, each rupee spent will achieve 37 rupees worth of social good.

Another intervention the researchers look at is micronutrient supplementation for pregnant women during ANC visits. The focus is on providing Vitamin A supplementation, iron, iodine, calcium, zinc and ORS. This very cheap intervention costing just hundreds of rupees per per beneficiary can avoid 133,787 cases of maternal anemia avoided, 47,196 avoided LBW babies, 425 avoided maternal deaths, 27,144 avoided preterm births, 1,900 avoided preterm deaths and 298 avoided stillbirths in Rajasthan. Each rupee spent targeting supplements to pregnant women in antenatal care would have benefits worth nearly 40 rupees.

Yearly impact of micronutrient supplements for pregnant women during ANC visits

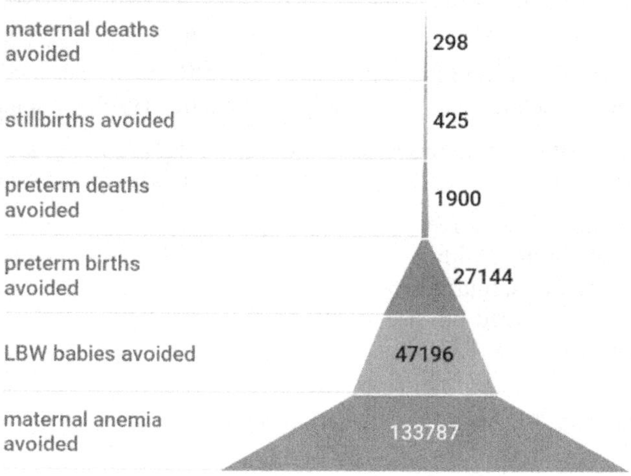

The researchers also look at interpersonal counselling for behaviour change. Diarrhoea is a significant cause of deaths among children under 5 years of age in Rajasthan. Low socioeconomic status, poor maternal literacy, inadequate breastfeeding, malnutrition, poor sanitation and hygiene practices of the mother or the caretaker are the major determinants of diarrheal diseases. A six-year intervention which includes counselling for breastfeeding and counselling for complementary feeding and hand washing will help to avoid a lot of illness and some deaths related to diarrhoea. Every rupee spent will yield more than 40 rupees in benefits to society.

Seldom in life are the benefits of simple, cheap policies so obvious and clear-cut: the new evidence points unambiguously to massive benefits from prioritizing closing gaps in access to nutrition interventions.

Interventions	BCR	Benefit	Cost
Education of mothers for breastfeeding, complementary feeding and hand-washing	43	₹54,134 /mother	₹1,245 /mother
Micronutrients for pregnant women at ANC visits	37	₹23,453 /mother	₹637 /mother
Supplementary food for mother and child	7	₹81,202 /beneficiary	₹11,532 /beneficiary
Package of nutrition based interventions	6	₹91,577 /beneficiary	₹14,144 /beneficiary
Community based treatment of children with severe acute malnutrition (SAM) using ready-to-use therapeutic food (RUTF)	5	₹46,951 /child	₹9,395 /child

Total costs and benefits are discounted at 5%

POVERTY: EVALUATING THE CHOICES TO HELP

In recent times, microcredit schemes have been presented as a panacea, attracting billions of rupees around the world. However, a series of trials have now shown that microcredit doesn't do much good – often not even increasing average incomes, and schemes can bury the poor in debt.

Subsidized crop insurance is another direct approach designed to help generate more income for the poorest of farmers by making agriculture less risky. But how useful is this approach? Munshi Sulaiman, Research Director of Save the Children International with Michael Murigi of the University of Sydney, analytically weigh up the costs and benefits of this along with other direct approaches to poverty.

Pradhan Mantri Fasal Bima Yojana (PMFBY) is the most recent—and most comprehensive—crop insurance model, launched in 2016 and reaching some 39 million farmers. Typically, the insurance premium is almost entirely paid by the central and state governments. In Rajasthan as an example, the researchers find that PMFBY, if expanded, will cost around 51,138 crore rupees.

This expenditure generates a number of benefits, including the actual insurance pay-outs, and allows farmers to take higher risks on more valuable crops that rely on bigger levels of rainfall. The insurance safety net means fewer suicides and less malnutrition for farming families.

While protecting farmers from income shocks is an important outcome on its own, the benefit of insurance coverage on farmers risk taking behavior, investment decisions and impact on productivity are the major economic justification for subsidizing crop insurance.

In the long run, two-thirds of the benefits come from the pay-out and one-quarter from higher profits. In total, every rupee spent on the policy achieves societal good worth about ₹1.53 rupees in Rajasthan.

In this case, the direct approach to alleviating poverty by subsidizing insurance does achieve more than it costs, but it can hardly be said that it has dramatic returns.

Another approach is a direct response to poverty that combines very specific interventions in a way that has been shown to have an immediate and sustained impact on food consumption, income, savings as well as assets.

Eliminating extreme poverty depends critically on creating sustainable livelihoods for the economically active ultra-poor: households who are landless and primarily rely on casual work for their livelihoods. The success of a "Graduation Approach" in a number of countries has made it a critical tool in social protection schemes. More than forty countries are now implementing different versions of this model, at various scales.

This approach was forged by the world's largest non-governmental organization (NGO), BRAC, and is implemented at small scale by various NGOs in West Bengal, Andhra Pradesh, and Jharkhand.

This model follows a strict set of targeting criteria to reach the ultra-poor and provides time-bound support that usually lasts between 18 and 24 months. First, food or money is given to the poor to ease the stress of daily survival; second, beneficiaries are encouraged to start savings. Third, they are provided with livestock or other income-generating assets. Following this, there is training provided in both technical skills and life skills. Finally, beneficiaries are provided with health support.

Each intervention costs more than ₹25,000, with half of this spent on the asset and food. Reaching 30% of poor households would cost ₹1,135 crore. Based on long-term studies from West Bengal, the increase in annual household consumption, savings and assets will mean every rupee spent will achieve at least ₹3.50 of social benefits and possibly even ₹6 – making it two- to three-times more effective as farmer insurance subsidies.

Cost-benefit ratio assuming different time horizon of the consumption effects of poverty graduation programs

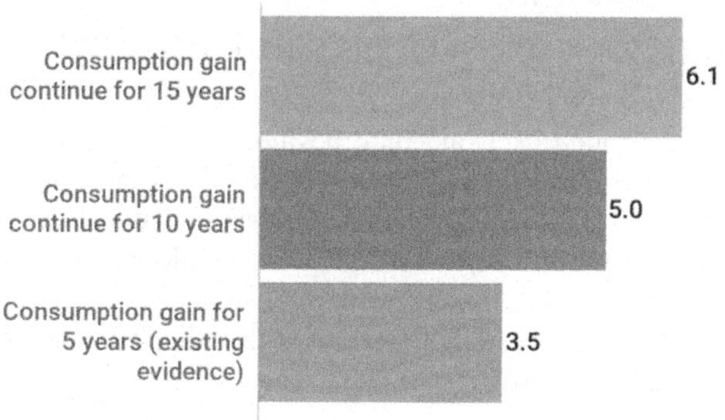

Interventions	BCR	Benefit	Cost
Ultra-poor graduation including asset transfer, health services and coaching (for 30% of all poor households)	3.5	₹4,014.8 crore	₹1,133.5 crore
Subsidised crop insurance until 2032	1.5	₹78,286.6 crore	₹51,138.5 crore

Total costs and benefits are discounted at 5%

UPSKILLING INDIA:
WHICH POLICIES SHOULD GET PRIORITY?

When India found itself in 103rd position in the recent World Economic Forum ranking of 130 nations on the preparedness of talent, it was just another indication of the skills challenge. In just five years, the Government's Skill Gap Analysis Report estimates that an extra 40 crore workers need to be skilled, reskilled or upskilled. The current official estimate is that slightly more than half a crore people are being trained annually.

Mansi Arora, Rajesh Chakrabarti, and Kushal Sagar Prakash from Sunay Policy Advisory have undertaken an analysis of three skills policies.

In Rajasthan, the skills challenge is clear: As per National Skill Development Corporation (NSDC) by 2022 Rajasthan will have a workforce of around 480 lakh with around 98 percent of that to be either fully or partially un-skilled. By 2022 Rajasthan will need about 11 percent of the total labour demanded to be fully skilled.

Rajasthan was one of the pioneer states to setup a skills mission by the name of Rajasthan Mission on Livelihoods, in 2004. The Rajasthan Skills and Livelihoods Corporation is executing various schemes and programmes. In 2015-16 Rajasthan Skill and Livelihoods Development Corporation (RSLDC) set up 300 new skill development centres in private public partnership (PPP) model, with a capacity to train 22,000. Between 2014-17, Department of Skills, Employment and Entrepreneurship of Rajasthan skilled more than 6 lakh youth.

The new research can help policy-makers by focusing on one important question: what is achieved with each additional rupee spent by AP on each skills policy?

The first policy examined is the provision of loan assistance to small and medium enterprises (SMEs) to encourage expansion and job creation. This may seem a roundabout route to up-skilling, but as a powerhouse of SMEs (like many Indian states), Rajasthan can create jobs by supporting their growth and development.

Research suggests that every rupee of loan will increase SME profit by about 0.89 rupees. Factoring borrowing costs, administration fees and default rates, it costs 16 rupees for every 100 rupees loaned. The researchers conclude that each rupee would generate benefits to the economy worth 5.6 rupees – a solid return on investment.

Costs and benefits of providing bank credit to MSMEs

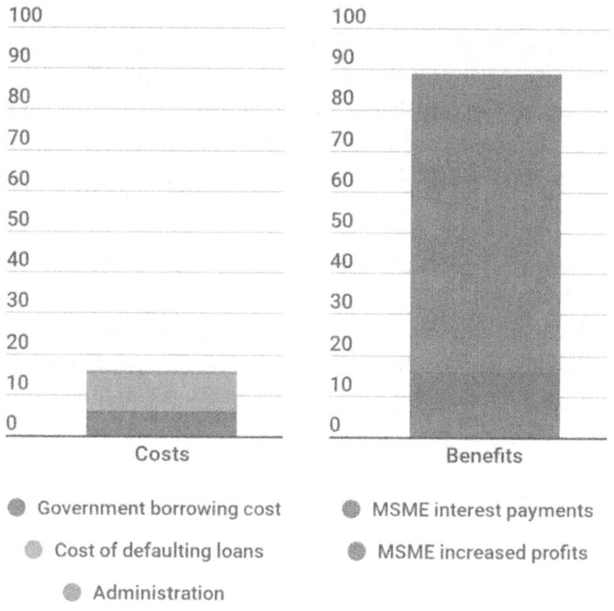

But to compete on a global stage, Rajasthan needs direct up-skilling policies. One approach studied is apprenticeship schemes that combine vocational education with work-based learning. For the employer, the cost is ₹1.5 lakhs, including salary, supervision, training, and administration. The government spends another ₹0.2 lakhs reimbursing employers, and on marketing. The individual misses out on about ₹0.22 lakhs in income during the apprenticeship. The total cost to everyone involved for a one-year apprenticeship is approximately ₹1.9 lakh.

The employee receives a substantial income increase over their working life, worth about ₹6.5 lakhs. The employer benefits to the tune of ₹2.2 lakhs, by having a more productive and job-ready workforce, increased revenue, and savings from having to recruit. Total benefits are ₹8.7 Lakh. Every rupee, therefore, spent on a year-long apprenticeship program is worth 4.5 rupees to the Rajasthan economy.

Finally, the authors look at expanding the current vocational training program to incentivize more people to join. This is job-specific, technical and hands-on. A similar analysis is undertaken: this time, the cost for each apprenticeship, both public and private, is about ₹0.45 lakh, forty percent of which represents foregone earnings.

The results show that an individual will earn ₹1.8 lakh more than an equivalent individual without vocational training over their lifetime. (This accounts for expected income growth as well as changing workforce participation and unemployment). The analysis reveals that benefits to society are 4-times higher than the costs.

Cost breakdown of training program vs. apprenticeship

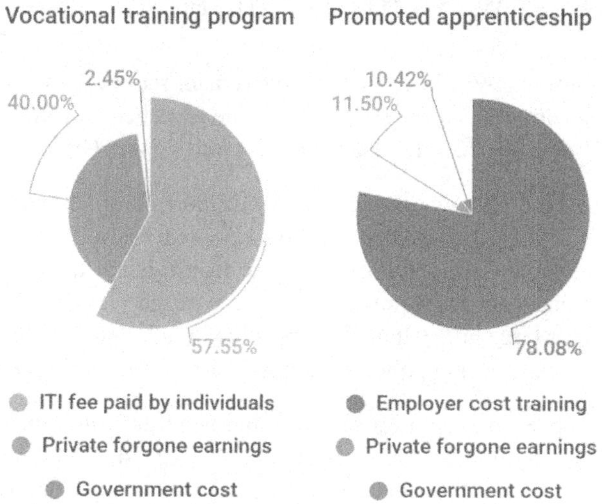

This research highlights the case for Rajasthan to invest more in expanding access vocational training programs –and the need to study the costs and benefits of skills policy options across India.

Interventions	BCR	Benefit	Cost
Apprenticeship	4.5	₹872,633 /individual	₹191,906 /individual
Vocational training	4.0	₹183,396 /individual	₹45,616 /individual
Credit support to MSME	6	89% of credit	16% of credit

Total costs and benefits are discounted at 5%

SOCIAL HOUSING: THE BEST WAYS TO HELP THE POOR

On assuming power in 2014, the Government set out to improve housing conditions for the urban poor, and launched Housing for All (HFA) by 2022 - 'Pradhan Mantri Awas Yojana Urban'.

New analysis examines the efficiency of three possible paths to achieve this goal. It shows that some approaches are stronger than others, and the result can help the Housing and Urban Affairs Department to examine the delivery of the HFA by 2022 agenda for large cities. It also prompts the broader question as to whether non-housing policies might better help the urban poor.

The comprehensive report on costs and benefits from housing policies is written by Amitabh Kundu, Distinguished Fellow at the Research and Information System for Developing Countries and Arjun Kumar, Visiting Fellow at the Institute for Human Development.

The first approach examined is Beneficiary-led Construction (BLC), where households with land or a house can claim a subsidy of ₹1.5 lakh for construction or an extension. This initiative is effectively driven by the beneficiaries. Costs include land and construction, and managing and supervising the construction. The benefits are many – like better living quarters, better health and better opportunity for a family to live together. All of these – and more – benefits are explicitly priced through the increased market value of the property.

In large cities in Rajasthan, the total cost of building a 300 sq. feet house is estimated under this scheme at ₹8.32 lakh, while Drs Kundu and Kumar find that the benefit – the increased market price – works out at nearly ₹9.95 lakh. Each rupee creates benefits worth a little more than one rupee.

The second approach is the Affordable Housing in Partnership (AHP) scheme, where projects are undertaken by public and private sectors in partnership, and 35 percent of houses are to be reserved for the economically weaker. This is a "supply-side" intervention to be led by private developers. The total cost of constructing a 300 sq. feet house under AHP in large cities in Rajasthan is estimated at about ₹6.3 lakh, with construction accounting for more than half. In addition to the market price rise, there is also a profit gained by the builder, which should be considered as part of the benefits to society, but given less weight because the builder will be in a different income group than poor beneficiaries.

The new analysis shows that total benefits to society come to nearly ₹9.49 lakh, so this achieves more than BLC, at about 1.5 rupees for each rupee spent.

The final approach examined by Drs Kundu and Kumar is In-situ Slum Redevelopment (ISSR), which leverages the land currently locked by slums, and involves re-housing slum dwellers in better accommodation in the same place, with the participation of private developers. This has no land cost, as the land is effectively already occupied. Consequently, the only costs are those of construction; internal and external infrastructure; community mobilization; project management; and providing transit accommodation.

Under this approach, the cost of a 300 sq. feet house in a large city in Rajasthan comes to just over ₹4 lakh. In addition to the market price rise, slum dwellers get additional benefits, including a reduction in death and healthcare spending, along with time savings because of access to basic amenities, especially water and sanitation.

Taking this into account, the approach generates benefits worth nearly ₹9 lakh, so each rupee achieves more than two rupees in benefits.

₹ lakh costs and benefits per 300 sq. feet house

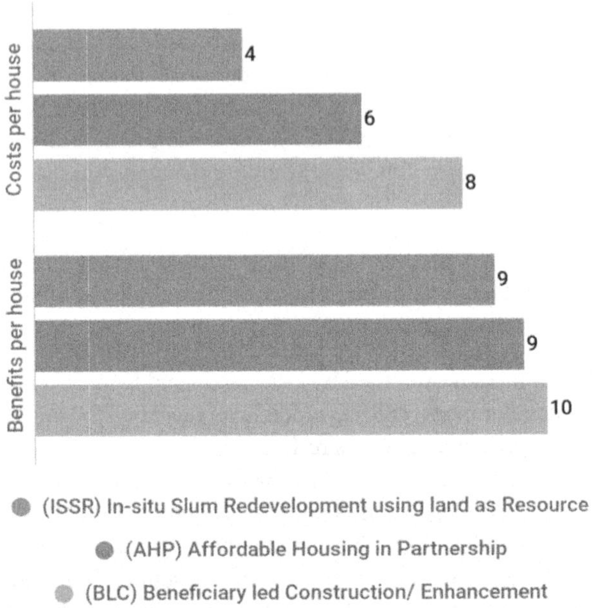

What are the lessons? For the Housing and Urban Affairs Department, it seems clear that among social housing approaches, ISSR should be top priority to achieve the most.

But there is perhaps a broader lesson, too. Other policies helping the urban poor—such as investment in improved Tuberculosis screening and treatment, or improved water and sanitation access—that generate many, many-times more rupees of benefits, for every rupee spent.

Having a safe, secure home provides dignity and protection against life shocks, and is a noble, important goal for government to deliver; but if the goal is to help the urban poor as effectively as possible, governments should consider all of the data, including this economic evidence.

Interventions	BCR	Benefit	Cost
In-situ Slum Redevelopment using land as Resource (ISSR)	2.2	₹8.92 lakhs per house	₹4.05 lakhs per house
Affordable Housing in Partnership (AHP)	1.5	₹9.49 lakhs per house	₹6.39 lakhs per house
Beneficiary led Construction/ Enhancement (BLC)	1.2	₹9.95 lakhs per house	₹8.32 lakhs per house

Total costs and benefits are estimated for a 300 square feet house and discounted at 5%

Enhancing Rajasthan's Trade Competitiveness

Free trade provides the greatest opportunity to improve human welfare, and has already helped lift more than a billion people out of poverty over the past quarter-century. India is transforming, thanks to its strong performance selling products and services around the globe.

But what interventions, at a state level, can do the most to ensure Indian exports are globally competitive?

Dr. Amitendu Palit of the National University of Singapore provides answers.

The study using cost-benefit analysis looks at what policies would help the state improve even more—and reveals that some policies are much better than others.

Rajasthan is India's largest state in land area and is a leading producer of agricultural commodities. While exports are natural advantages of coastal states, a hinterland state like Rajasthan can accelerate exports if equipped with appropriate infrastructure, particularly logistics capacities. One of the disadvantages that Rajasthan has traditionally suffered from is lack of adequate infrastructure for transporting goods to seaports. The state is working on increasing competitiveness of its exports by augmenting modern infrastructure and export-oriented capacities and reducing costs of doing business. Its objective is to increase its share in national exports from 2% right now to much higher levels.

The researchers examine three policy interventions for implementation for enhancing the competitiveness of Rajasthan's exports. Rajasthan being a part of the transport connectivity landscape of the Delhi-Mumbai Industrial Corridor (DMIC), the interventions include development of an inland container depot (ICD) and container terminal; a free trade warehousing zone

(FTWZ); and scientific facilities for testing and certifying organic food exports.

Rajasthan currently has three ICDs at Jodhpur, Jaipur and Kathuwas. Another ICD equipped with a container terminal with strong multimodal transport linkages would encourage movement of goods and exporters by bringing down logistics costs. The importance of the proposed intervention for Rajasthan increases in the light of the upcoming Delhi Mumbai Industrial Corridor (DMIC). The proposed ICD – located in close proximity to Jaipur and DMIC – is visualised to augment the state's logistics capacity.

This would cost ₹3,137 crores, while the benefits are estimated to be worth ₹4,853 crores to Rajasthan. This means that the benefits are 1.5 times the costs.

Yearly ₹ crore costs and revenue of inland container depot

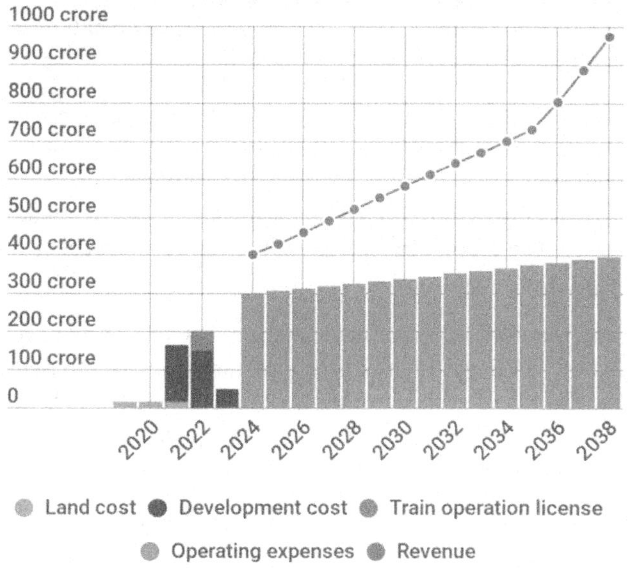

The second proposal studied is a FTWZ of around 125 acre, i.e. roughly 50 hectares, located close to the DMIC for facilitating crucial backward and forward linkages. This is an intervention that would take time to break even and should, therefore, be posited in the right geography for ensuring optimal returns.

While land purchase costs are staggered over 3 years, development costs for the facility, computed on the basis of available warehouse development cost estimates and staggered over four years, are estimated much higher at an aggregate of ₹500 crore. Operating costs are high. Total costs of this intervention are estimated at ₹3,007 crores.

Revenues are computed on the basis of indicative warehousing charges for FTWZs. It is assumed that there would be 70% utilisation of capacity based on continuing improvement in business conditions and good demand. Annual revenue of ₹275 crore from the first year of operations – i.e. the 7th year– and a 5% increase in revenues each year is expected. Total benefits estimated from this intervention come to ₹2,736 crores, so the intervention costs more than it achieves.

The final intervention involves establishing a laboratory equipped with latest scientific testing facilities for certifying quality standards of organic food exports from Rajasthan to the EU, North America, and other major markets in Asia, including Australia. The laboratory will greatly enhance prospects of organic food exports

The intervention is cheaper than others, at ₹50 crores, and expectations of additional Rajasthan exports are calculated based on the benchmark of current estimates of organic food exports from India for 2015-16. The total benefits are estimated at 75 crores, so every rupee achieves 1.5 rupees of benefits.

It is important that Rajasthan picks the best opportunities to continue to compete globally.

Interventions	BCR	Benefit	Cost
Scientific testing and certification facilities for organic product exports (Time horizon 10 years)	1.5	₹75 crore	₹50 crore
Development of an inland container depot and container terminal (Time horizon 20 years)	1.5	₹4,853 crore	₹3,137 crore
Establishing a Free Trade Ware-housing Zone (FTWZ) (Time horizon 10 years)	0.9	₹ 2,736 crore	₹3,007 crore

Total costs and benefits are discounted at 5%

Battling Tuberculosis: Lifting Rajasthan's health ranking and saving thousands of lives every year

For Rajasthan and for every state, managing tuberculosis (TB) is especially important because in addition to claiming many lives, it has a cascading effect, since one case treated saves others from being infected. Managing this killer disease and especially the costly and increasing multi-drug resistant variant will mean the health system will have more money to tackle other health priorities.

The national strategic plan for TB elimination, launched in 2017, set out a renewed ambition to control and eradicate the disease. The crucial question is how to make this happen.

Nimalan Arinaminpathy, a senior lecturer in Mathematical Epidemiology at the School of Public Health, Imperial College London, has explored two options that would improve the response to TB, and thus lift Rajasthan's health performance.

Dr. Arinaminpathy's first proposal is to increase the quality of TB care in the private sector, by creating a 'Public Private Support Agency' (PPSA), also mentioned as one of the critical components in the NSP 2017-25 (National Strategic Plan).

Mumbai and Patna have already engaged such agencies to identify and enlist private providers for case notification and follow up, supported by public funds and overseen by the national TB programme.

Lifting the standard of TB care in the private sector is critical, since the National Strategic Plan (NSP) 2017-25 identifies that well over half of TB infected first go to private clinics. Poor compliance with patient management strategies and use of inaccurate tests can delay diagnosis, thus permitting ongoing transmission, while a general lack of treatment support means that many private patients do not complete the 6-month standard TB regimen.

This leads to poorer outcomes than in the public sector, and increases the risk of multi-drug-resistance.

Importantly, unlike earlier public-private mix approaches, private providers would continue to manage TB patients. This is crucial to engage the private providers, so they don't just see the purpose of the PPSA to 'divert' the patient to the public sector.

To estimate the cost, Dr. Arinaminpathy uses pilot study costs. He conservatively estimates that it will only manage to reach half of TB patients. In this scenario, the total cost would be 304 crore per year between now and 2050. This would save 3,322 lives every year on average, or 11.5% of the deaths that might otherwise have occurred.

Every rupee would generate 117 rupees of benefits. That's a remarkable 'return on investment'.

The second intervention adds improved case-finding. Currently, TB services largely wait for symptomatic patients to show up to a clinic. Case-finding aims to go into the community to detect TB cases. This would diagnose patients earlier, shorten the period over which they are infectious, and reach under-served populations. As in the NSP 2017-25, the research sets urban slums as a priority area: they have just 10% of the population but account for one-quarter of the TB burden. This is crucial for cities which have a higher proportion of urban slums – around 40 % according to the 2011 census.

In these areas, under the proposal screening would be conducted once per year for TB using X-rays. Possible cases would be diagnosed using accurate, rapid tests. If positive, people would be referred to the public sector for treatment. This intervention would be supported, staffed and implemented by the national TB programme.

In combination with private sector engagement, the cost for the first years would be around ₹42 crores. Crucially, less TB will cut multi-drug resistant cases by up to 80%. Since these cases are much more expensive, it will mean much lower costs in later years, opening up opportunities for more spending on other health care challenges.

Yearly costs and cost savings in ₹ crores from improving private sector TB care and increasing active case finding

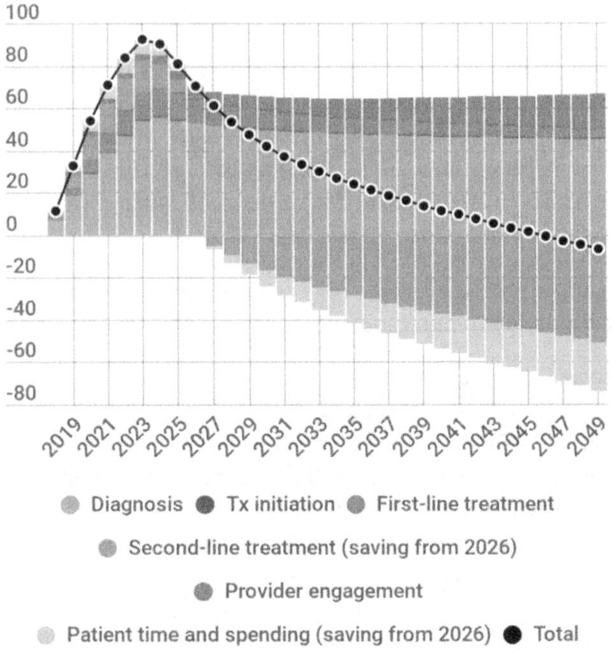

Case-finding would avert an average of 4,980 TB deaths per year, or 17.2% of deaths that might otherwise have occurred. The analysis shows that each rupee spent generates a return on investment worth 180 rupees.

The analysis highlights two compelling approaches that could strongly boost Rajasthan's health performance, ensuring not only that thousands of lives are saved, but that resources are well-allocated so that the system runs better for all.

Interventions	BCR	Benefit	Cost
Improve private sector TB care	179	₹54,541 crores	₹304.00 cores
Improve private sector TB care and implement active case finding	117	₹81,959 crores	₹699.22 crores

Total costs and benefits are discounted at 5%

URBAN GROWTH: HOW UDAIPUR CAN KEEP PACE WITH INFRASTRUCTURE NEEDS

Cities are, in many ways, the future of India. The number of metropolitan cities with a population higher than 1 million jumped from 35 in 2001 to 50 in 2011, and is expected to reach 87 by 2031. Today, 40 crore people call an Indian metropolis home; that will double by 2050.

This swift growth places huge pressure on infrastructure that in very few cases was ever designed with so many people in mind.

A major report in 2010 found that the duration of water supply in Indian cities ranges from 1-6 hours; only about 21 percent of waste water generated is treated; and less than one-third of municipal solid waste is segregated.

Gagan Nigam of IL&FS with Priyesh Shukla and Manish Gupta of PDCOR, studies what this would mean for Udaipur in Rajasthan.

The researchers first look at the costs and benefits of providing 100% sewerage and wastewater treatment to the major city of each state. In Udaipur, presently less than half of the city is covered by the sewerage network. Ensuring 100% coverage and provisions for wastewater treatment would cost ₹1,300 crore, with most being operating expenditure. This would benefit more than 10 lakh residents and help maintain the cleanliness of the Ahar river, polluted by sewage. The health benefits, alone would, put into financial terms, be worth ₹1,400 crore of the entire ₹1,500 crore benefits.

Greater returns would come, for every rupee spent, by focusing on solid waste management.

Udaipur generates approximately 120 tons per day of municipal solid waste. Door-to-door collection services cover just 20%; moreover, segregation and processing are not carried out at all. Instead, all waste is sent to an open dumpsite.

Achieving 100% collection, transportation, and management with minimal amounts going to the landfill would cost around ₹500 crore, including both capital expenditure and operating spending.

There would be considerable benefits. Many of these can be identified by working out what citizens would pay to have improved solid waste management. There are also improvements in land value, and money gained from selling compost and Refuse derived fuel. In total, these benefits would be worth ₹900 crore to Udaipur including estimated land value savings of over ₹150 crore and revenue close to ₹50 crore through sale of compost and RDF.

Finally, focusing on the urban water supply would mean even better returns. Udaipur has piped water network coverage of close to 80%. However, more than half of the approximately 78,000 connections are dilapidated, and need replacement.

Urban 24x7 piped water total costs and benefits

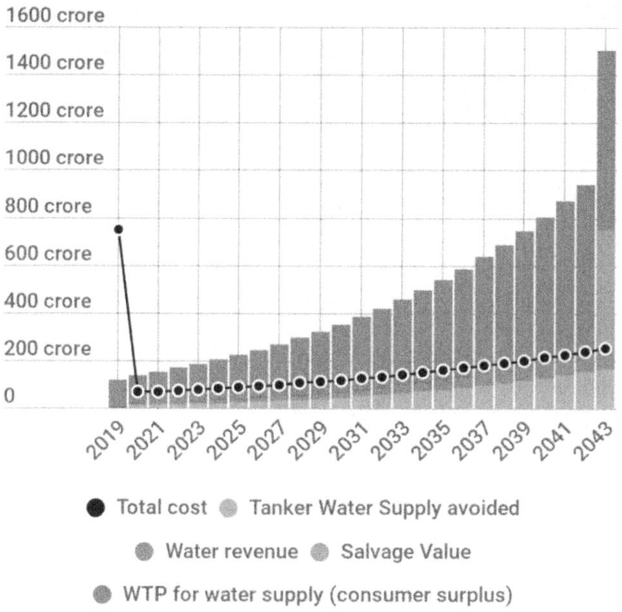

So supplying 100% coverage would mean replacing many

existing distribution pipes, and the costs would come to ₹2,300 crore. Citizens would not only have health benefits, but would also be able to avoid the cost of creating bore well and pump maintenance to extract ground water. These advantages, plus revenues to the city, would mean benefits add up to ₹5,300 crore.

This suggests a return on investment worth nearly three rupees for Rajasthan.

What is clear is that India's cities are burgeoning, and significant infrastructure needs to be developed to meet unmet demand and to keep pace with the growth.

Interventions	BCR	Benefit	Cost
Urban 24x7 piped water supply	2.3	₹5,276 crore	₹2,320 crore
Urban waste collection 100 percent	2.0	₹906 crore	₹461 crore
Urban sewerage and wastewater treatment 100 percent	1.1	₹1,489 crore	₹1,298 crore

Total costs and benefits estimated over a 25-year time horizon and discounted at 5%

Analysing Water and Sanitation Options for the State

Diarrheal disease caused nearly 1.7 million deaths globally in 2016. Nearly 0.8 million of these deaths occurred in India of which 90% were due to unsafe drinking water, sanitation and hygiene according to estimates by the Global Burden of Disease 2016. In Rajasthan over 47 thousand deaths were caused by diarrheal disease and intestinal infections (mainly typhoid and paratyphoid) in 2016, constituting 8.7% of all deaths in the state.

To address these issues, four interventions are analyzed by economist Bjorn Larsen. Benefits and costs are presented as a ratio of annualized benefits and annualized costs over the expected useful life of each intervention.

Over 85% of households in Rajasthan had access to an improved drinking water source in 2015-16, up from 82% in 2005-06 according to the National Family Health Survey

Only 6% of households practiced point-of-use (POU) treatment of their drinking water in 2005-06, mainly by filtering. Moreover, as much of a quarter of the population in Rajasthan had more than 30 minutes round-trip to their drinking water source in 2005-06 (NFHS 3), particularly affecting women and children.

Providing urban households without an improved drinking water source with piped water to dwelling, or rural households with a tube well/borehole would cost around ₹1,429 per household. This includes initial capital cost of piped water supply or tube well/borehole and annual operations and maintenance cost. For urban areas the annualized cost of improved drinking water supply is estimated at ₹48 crores per year and for rural areas annualized cost is estimated at ₹464 crores per year.

The intervention would benefit about 3.6 million households. The largest benefits are avoided mortality and productivity benefits in terms of time savings from water source closer to dwelling.

Households covered by proposed water interventions

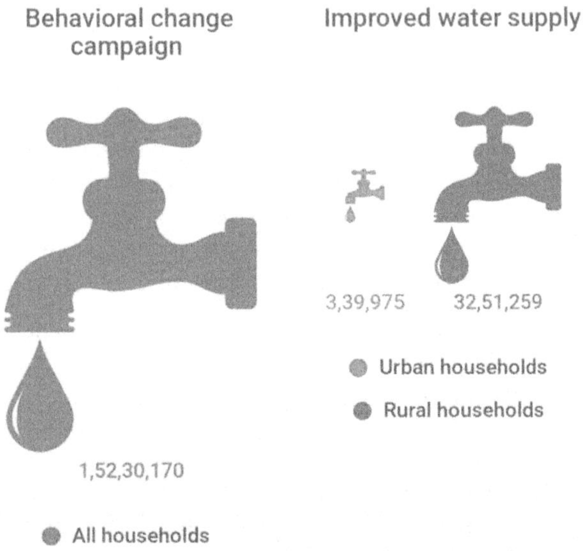

For urban intervention annualized benefits are estimated at ₹265 crores per year and for rural area annualized benefits are estimated at ₹2097 crores per year.

It would avert nearly 1,100 deaths and 2.2 million cases of diarrheal illness. In monetary terms, benefits in urban areas are 5.5 rupees for every rupee spent, and 4.5 rupees in rural areas.

Only a little over 6% of households in Rajasthan practiced appropriate methods of point-of-use (POU) treatment of drinking water a decade ago, compared to over 20% nationwide in India according to the NFHS 3 (2005-06).

A behavioural change campaign that promotes household POU treatment of drinking water with a filter would cost ₹363 crores, targeting 1.5-3 million households (the cost for them to start POU treatment by filtering of drinking water has been factored). It is estimated that about 1,900-3,900 deaths and 3.9-7.9 million cases of diarrheal illness will be averted per year. Total value of the health and productivity benefits of the intervention is estimated at ₹1,470 crores per year. The benefits are worth 4 rupees for every rupee spent.

About 52% of households in Rajasthan had a sanitary toilet facility in 2015 according to the Swachhta Status Report 2016. The next intervention targets 95% household coverage with improved, non-shared sanitation.

Households covered by proposed sanitation interventions

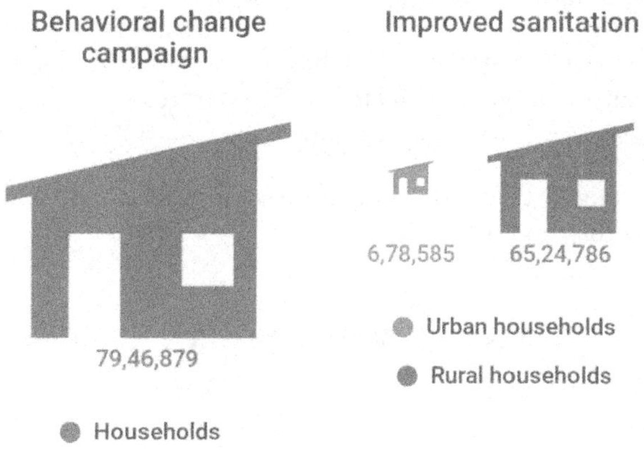

Costs of household sanitation include initial capital cost, periodic emptying of pit or septic tank (once in 5 years), annual operations and maintenance cost, cost or time for cleaning of sanitation facility, and cost of sanitation promotion programs by the government. The annualized cost per household is estimated at 5,500 to 8,200 (with urban households being cheaper than rural households). It is estimated that 13,600 deaths and 28 million cases of diarrheal illness will be averted per year due to this intervention.

The total value of the annualized health and productivity benefits of the intervention is estimated at ₹2,651 crores for urban areas and ₹23,960 crores for rural areas. Benefits are worth 4.8 times costs in urban areas, and 6.6 times in rural areas.

Finally, the researcher looks at promotion of the use of sanitation facilities. The Swachhta Status Report 2016 found that 4.5% of household members continue to practice Open Defecation after construction of sanitation facility. NonThe intervention is a behavioral change campaign that promotes the consistent use of existing sanitation facilities.

The total annualized cost (both program and additional costs of improved water, etc) of this intervention is ₹125 crores. It is estimated cases of 40-80 deaths and about 83,000-167,000 cases of diarrheal illness will be averted per year.

The total value of the annualized health and productivity benefits of the intervention is estimated at ₹231 crores, so each rupee spent achieves nearly 2 rupees of benefits.

This highlights the range of different options for policy-makers, in both urban and rural areas.

Interventions	BCR	Benefit	Cost
Rural flush / pour-flush sanitation	6.6	₹23,961 crore / year	₹3,623.4 crore / year
Urban improved drinking water supply	5.5	₹265 crore / year	₹48.6 crore / year
Urban flush / pour-flush sanitation	4.8	₹2,652 crore / year	₹555.2 crore / year
Behavioural change for household treatment of drinking water	4.0	₹1,471 crore / year	₹363.8 crore / year
Rural improved drinking water supply	4.5	₹2,098 crore / year	₹464.5 crore / year
Behavioural change for use of existing sanitation facilities	1.9	₹232 crore / year	₹125.1 crore / year

Total costs and benefits estimated over a 25-year time horizon and discounted at 5%

Rajasthan Priorities
Eminent Panel Findings

The Rajasthan Priorities Eminent Panel comprises:

- Dr Bibek Debroy
- Professor Amitabh Mattoo
- Dr Alok Ray
- Dr Rathin Roy

The Eminent Panel sought to address the research proposals with a view to answering the question: *On which initiatives should additional resources be spent first?*

The Eminent Panel intends these findings to be informative not just to the Government of Rajasthan, but also to others, including NGOs and charitable organizations.

The panel examined the proposals in detail. Each proposal was discussed with its principal author. The panel was informed by Sector Expert Commentaries, and by Panel members' own critical appraisals and discussions on assumptions and methodology.

In ordering the proposals, the Eminent Panel was guided predominantly by consideration of social, economic and environmental costs and benefits.

The Eminent Panel acknowledged the difficulties that cost-benefit analysis must overcome, both in principle and as a practical matter, but agreed that the cost-benefit approach was a very important organizing method.

Each Eminent Panel member assigned his own ranking to proposals. The Eminent Panel's ranking was calculated by taking the median of individual rankings.

The Eminent Panel jointly endorses the median ordering as representing their agreed view.

Ranking of Proposals

The Eminent Panel considers and prioritizes specific proposals to respond to challenges. This is different from ranking the challenges themselves. A low ranking of a proposal does not mean that the problem it addresses should be considered unimportant.

The Ranking was calculated by taking the median of each Eminent Panel member's individual rankings. The Eminent Panel jointly endorses the median ordering as representing their agreed view. In due course, the Eminent Panel's individual commentaries shall be published in book form.

In setting priorities, the Eminent Panel has taken into account the strengths and weaknesses of the specific cost-benefit appraisals under review, and has given weight both to the institutional preconditions for success and to the demands of ethical or humanitarian importance.

Based on the costs and benefits of the solutions and their own assessment, the panel ranked the proposals, in descending order of desirability, as follows:

Rank	Proposal
1	Improve private sector TB care
2	Improve private sector TB care and active case finding
3	Education for complementary feeding and handwashing
4	Package of nutrition based interventions
5	Supplementary food for mother and child
6	Improve land records digitisation
7	Micronutrients for pregnant women at ANC visits
8	Secondary prevention of cardiovascular disease
9	Energy storage in commercial buildings - water
10	E-mandis to reduce middle-men superprofits
11	Immunization camps in lagging districts
12	Certified seed production

13	Expand urban ambulance network
14	Expand rural ambulance network
15	Diabetes screening and treatment
16	Zig-zag brick kiln technology to reduce air pollution
17	Mass media breastfeeding promotion and counseling
18	Vertical shaft brick kiln technology to reduce air pollution
19	Urban sewerage and wastewater treament 100 percent
20	Treatment for children with severe acute malnutrition
21	Tablets to reduce anaemia in adolescent girls
22	Conditional cash transfer for ANC visits
23	Urban waste collection 100 percent
24	Build warehouses, storage and cold chain
25	Renovation of traditional water harvesting
26	Urban 24x7 piped water supply
27	Expand water use efficient irrigation
28	Expand Aadhaar based payments for MGNREGA
29	Improved maternal and neonatal health care
30	Improved drinking water supply - urban
31	Self-help groups against domestic violence
32	Improved drinking water supply - rural
33	Behavioural change for household treatment of drinking water
34	Family planning for unmet need
35	Community mobilisation against domestic violence
36	Cash transfer for girls' secondary school enrolment
37	Well-structured incentives to teachers
38	Connect rural households to national fibre optic network
39	Cash transfer for girls' secondary school enrolment
40	Group and teach children at the right level
41	Direct non-monetary incentives to reduce child marriage
42	Subsidised apprenticeships
43	Bicycle transfer for girls' secondary school enrolment
44	Vocational training program
45	Improved mobile phone advisory

46	Computer assisted learning at the right level
47	Soil health card
48	Cervical cancer screening and treatment
49	Crop diversification
50	In-situ slum redevelopment
51	Private-public affordable housing projects
52	Energy efficient agricultural water pumps
53	Indoor air pollution: Improved biomass cookstoves promotion
54	Organic products certification for export
55	Free trade warehousing zone
56	Inland container terminal
57	Upgrade agricultural power distribution
58	Behavioural change for use of existing sanitation facilities
59	Expand poverty graduation and livelihood programs
60	Breast cancer screening and treatment
61	Double teacher-pupil ratio
62	Expand skill training for women
63	Expand crop insurance coverage
64	Mental health counselling in schools
65	Indoor air pollution: Free LPG connection to poor households
66	Subsidised do-it-yourself extension and construction
67	Expanding the grid to unserved population
68	Cash incentives to attend pre-school classes in AWCs
69	Hire local teachers to improve pre-school classes in AWCs
70	Toilet provision for girls' secondary school enrolment
71	Flush / Pour-flush sanitation - rural
72	Training of teachers
73	Diesel microgrids to unserved population
74	Flush / Pour-flush sanitation - urban
75	Start-up incubator support
76	Credit support to micro, small and medium enterprises
77	Farmer loan waivers

Notes on some Eminent Panel Rankings

• **Subsidized apprenticeships and Vocational training program:** The Panel notes that in implementation, these two interventions can complement each other, and the best approach may be a package one, rather than a silo approach being undertaken.

• **Cash transfers for Child Marriage:** The Panel notes that it is important to not only incentivize school enrolment, but also incentivize retention and graduation.

• **Credit support to micro, small and medium enterprises:** An update from the author to the Panel clarified that this intervention involves providing a credit facility and business management hand-holding for MSMEs; it is this full intervention that the Panel has ranked.

• **Energy efficient agricultural water pumps and Upgrade agricultural power distribution:** The Panel makes the note that these interventions are bankable.

Commentary on the Rankings
by Dr Bibek Debroy

Chairman of the Economic Advisory Council to the Prime Minister (EAC-PM) and Member of NITI Aayog, the think-tank of the Indian Government. Dr. Bibek Debroy was educated in Ramakrishna Mission School, Narendrapur; Presidency College, Kolkata; Delhi School of Economics and Trinity College, Cambridge. He was awarded the 'Padma Shri' (the fourth-highest civilian honour in India) in 2015. In 2016, he was awarded the Lifetime Achievement Award by US-India Business Summit. He has worked in following Professional bodies: Presidency College, Kolkata (1979-83); Gokhale Institute of Politics and Economics, Pune (1983-87); Indian Institute of Foreign Trade, Delhi (1987-93); as The Director of a Ministry of Finance/UNDP project on legal reforms (1993-98); Department of Economic Affairs (1994-95); National Council of Applied Economic Research (1995-96); Rajiv Gandhi Institute for Contemporary Studies (1997-2005); PHD Chamber of Commerce and Industry (2005-06); Centre for Policy Research (2007-2015).He has authored/edited several books, papers and popular articles and has also been a Consulting/Contributing Editor with several newspapers.

The Rajasthan Consensus Project did an excellent job of bringing together various ideas focused on improving the socio-economic status of the State of Rajasthan on one platform, using a well-thought out methodology. The Benefit-Cost analysis methodology, based on maximizing social returns from limited resources has reasonable utility in making policy decisions. Scarcity of resources, and administrative capacity, is a key driver of policy decisions and thus, the idea of ranking policy options in a scientific manner allows for best utilization of available resources. I wish to compliment the efforts put in by the researchers to propose and defend their interventions that followed this framework. The presentations made by various researchers proved critical in analyzing the relevance of their ideas. Further, the discussions with fellow panel members on the merits and demerits of various policy interventions was a very fruitful exercise, as it helped in gaining different perspectives and thoughts on the applicability of various proposals. I commend the Rajasthan Consensus team for designing a robust process that proved effective in ranking the 79 interventions on various critical themes. Such an exercise for other Indian states will add immense value to decision making at regional and local levels.

Rajasthan's geographical size and cultural diversity makes it a complex state to govern. Therefore, the interventions to improve the state of affairs have to be carefully designed so that they factor in the ground realities and the work being pursued by the government. In my judgement, one major factor behind ranking interventions was their specificity to Rajasthan. It's true that a lot of problems can be similar across India, but the solutions have to be targeted taking the local context into consideration. For instance, the idea of using an improved technology for operating brick kilns in Rajasthan aptly understood that such kilns use outdated technology in Rajasthan and provided a clear solution for the target districts with high density of such kilns. The intervention targeted the problem of outdoor air pollution that isn't uncommon in other Indian states, however, it went the extra mile of identifying one of the major sources of outdoor pollution in Rajasthan and addressed it with appropriate interventions. At the same time, an intervention that proposed building an Inland Container Terminal lacked details on where to build, what industries to target, etc. Missing such details not only undermines the understanding of prevailing problems, but also places a big question mark against the execution viability of such interventions. These are two examples of how specificity in the intervention design adds to its merit, or does not.

Another aspect that greatly helped interventions achieve a higher rank was their ability to complement the ongoing initiatives in Rajasthan. For instance, an intervention that proposed providing LPG cylinders to target indoor air pollution completely discounted the fact that the current scheme (being spearheaded by the Union government) along similar lines has covered a lot of ground. If the researchers had taken cognizance of this reality, the inclination to propose alternatives to LPG would have gone down. Further, if one advocates an initiative to reinvent the wheel by undoing recent progress, there wouldn't be much excitement in the government about implementing it. However, there were many interventions that rightly understood the existing government initiatives and the utility of building on them. The intervention advocating Ambulance Network expansion in rural and urban areas rightly analyzed the need to add on the current network areas which are devoid them. A decent benefit-cost ratio for such an intervention would have a much higher appeal with the state government, which is ultimately responsible in implementing it.

On the calculation side, incorporating latest data to design interventions was key to merit a higher rank. This was also essential for researchers to arrive at more accurate benefit cost ratios. Old data not only contaminates the real utility of an intervention, but also corrodes the importance of a worthy intervention when it is proposed to the right stakeholders. To quote an extreme example, the benefit cost ratio that argued for providing toilets to all didn't incorporate that 100% household coverage has already been achieved in Rajasthan. The jump in sanitation coverage was achieved in a mere 3 years. Open Defecation Status for Rajasthan stands at 100% in 2018 as against 15% in 2015-16. These data are available in the public domain and the ignorance only eroded the real value proposition of the intervention focused on improving sanitation. Similar interventions that didn't account for such changes lost against those that did. Many interventions that did use latest data achieved a relatively higher rank. These interventions did a good job of filling in missing information as well. The assumptions made were practical and very close to ground realities. The intervention to link remaining MNREGA workers with Aadhar to enable direct transfer of wages did a decent job of factoring in the right and up to date data, thereby, making its benefit-cost ratio more accurate.

The ranking also factored in the novelty of ideas and their scalability in various parts of Rajasthan. It is on this parameter that interventions such as piped water supply for Udaipur, active case finding and treatment for Tuberculosis achieved higher ranks. Once again, on this parameter, Incubator Support to Start ups, Teacher training, etc. couldn't score well. This parameter along with the rigor of research, analysis and assumptions played a defining role in ranking all 79 interventions. Additionally, the broad sector that interventions were in were important as well. Policy areas that are critically linked to human development, such as health, education, and basic infrastructure always get importance over areas that have subtle long-term impact. However, this factor was only used to separate interventions which came too close to each other on other mentioned parameters.

As far as some of the top ranked interventions are concerned, they hit the right balance of all the parameters specified above. Fast tracking immunization in lagging districts, renovating traditional water harvesting structures (khadins) in western Rajasthan and subsidizing Energy Storage technologies all hit the right spots. Health, water and electricity (not just access but also adequacy) are the prime challenges for Rajasthan and deserve attention from the government. The said interventions have worked well in Rajasthan or similar geographies and did present a strong case for improving the existing scenario. The same is also true for interventions that targeted Tuberculosis and Nutrition. Not only are these important themes, but the interventions also presented a strong case for improving the status quo.

I will conclude by once again congratulating the India Consensus team for identifying and hand-holding various researchers in designing and evaluating various important interventions. I was especially impressed in the manner all interventions were methodically aligned, so that comparing them and ranking them was possible. This background work proved critical in debating the real merit of interventions with fellow panel members. I hope that the India Consensus Prioritization Project covers many more Indian States to strengthen policy decision making and enhance the pace of development.

Commentary on the Rankings
by Prof. Amitabh Mattoo

Advisor to the Chief Minister of Jammu and Kashmir, with the status of a Cabinet Minister; CEO and Honorary Director of the Australia India Institute at Delhi; and Professor of International Relations at the University of Melbourne. He is also a Professor of Disarmament Studies in Jawaharlal Nehru University. He has been a member of the National Security Advisory Board and a member of the National Knowledge Commission to the Prime Minister of India. Professor Amitabh Mattoo was Vice-Chancellor of the University of Jammu from 2002-2008. Recognizing his contribution to education and public life, the President of India honoured Professor Mattoo with the Padma Shri, one of India's highest civilian awards.

Rajasthan is the largest Indian state in terms of geographical area. (Census 2011, 2011) With varied terrain, livelihood, dispersed patterns of settlement and social identity in the state, the aim of this project, Rajasthan Priorities, was to generate policies in order to find the smartest solution to some of the most pressing development issues in the state. Studies were conducted across a wide range of verticals, covering policy areas from education, nutrition, and energy storage to water and sanitation – leading to extensive discussions with sector experts and stakeholders.

At the eminent panel conference, the economists presented benefit-cost analyses of the 79 possible interventions. These possible interventions were identified and analysed. The analysis was to determine the most cost effective, socially productive and energy efficient interventions for the state of Rajasthan. After rigorous and a robust academic debate, four eminent panel members including myself, prioritised the development interventions and policies that would best serve the state of Rajasthan.

The government of Rajasthan has implemented a large number of initiatives and schemes across various sectors for the benefit of the citizens of the state. However, the research conducted highlights that the state continues to face acute social and economic development challenges.

Two important areas where both empirical analysis and anecdotal evidence called for government policy intervention were

Nutrition and Tuberculosis and were thus prioritised amongst the top.

As suggested in the research paper titled, "Nutrition", the prevalence of malnutrition in Rajasthan is extremely high and it performs poorly compared to other Indian states. The intergenerational cycle of undernourishment is a concern for future prospects of its economic growth as it enters the most productive phase of demographic transition.

The presentation of this paper highlighted that the 5 proposed interventions were in line with the National Nutrition Mission of 2022. The paper with robust data analysis focused on identifying growth and development deficits in child health, mortality and the achievement of optimal learning outcomes that are cumulative and largely irreversible across the life cycle. All the interventions were inclusive and gender sensitive, rooted in community empowerment, and they valued and enhanced the contribution of Anganwadi workers.

The majority of pregnant women were anemic and consequently children were born with low birth weight, stunted growth, low prevalence of exclusive breastfeeding, the provision of essential health and nutrition inputs became the topmost priority. The cost-benefit analysis of the nutrition interventions presented in the paper had shown that there are sizeable benefits to be reaped. The, 'Package of nutrition based intervention', with a favourable BCR of 6 - Behaviour change counselling, supplementary food and micronutrient supplements will increase coverage by 10% resulting in avoiding 365 deaths and reduction in stunting by 20% in the population receiving the intervention.

Another intervention with an exceptionally high BCR and the one that was most coherent with existing literature and policies in the state was, 'Tuberculosis', and was ranked amongst the top 5. This intervention had a clear analysis of the problem and the possible solutions in terms of benefits and costs. Tuberculosis is a major global health challenge and India's recent National Strategic Plan (NSP) for TB elimination, launched in 2017, renews ambition for TB control. This paper on Tuberculosis which examines the Benefit Cost Ratios of two interventions, are introduced individually and as a combination, are quite timely and relevant. The premises of the study were fairly simple with a sustained landscape of engaging the private sector and active case finding. It provides a method for estimating the number of lives saved against the investments, and conversely gives a monetary value to the number of deaths averted, when more cases are detected early and notified; and supported during the course of treatment. This study may highlight the bigger picture and bring about a realization that efforts put in today, by reaching out to the private sector and by carrying out active case finding campaigns, have a measurable impact on preventing new TB cases, TB deaths and catastrophic costs, thereby ending TB in the near future.

Considering the detailed analysis of these research papers at the Eminent Panel Conference, along with the discussion on its practical implementation, 'Nutrition' and 'Tuberculosis, have been ranked in the top 5.

The discussions touched upon a wide range of policy areas, however many of the interventions were either already in progress or have been envisaged by the government. Some of the interventions were not coherent with current government data or structurally incompetent. A few of these interventions addressed the prevention of Child Marriage and the improvement of preschool education at Anganwadi centres. These have been ranked least effective.

The government of Rajasthan has already implemented a scheme of distribution of free bicycles – painted orange, in the various districts of Rajasthan. The success of this intervention is debatable. Toilet provision for girls to increase secondary school enrolment seems very arbitrary ideologically and the costs are too high to reap equivalent benefits.

Similarly, cash incentives for children to attend pre-school classes in AWCs seems a far-fetched idea when existing literature and similar interventions in other states have not yielded expected results. The paper itself claims that the quality of evidence for the cash transfer is 'limited'. It was discussed and recommended that the conditional cash transfers should be given post the completion of a student's academic degree.

Review of existing literature, broad stakeholder engagement, data driven analysis and detailed discussions at the conference formed the basis of our prioritizing these interventions that strike the right balance between economic and human development. The final rankings are the median outcome of the prioritisation given by the Eminent Panel.

COMMENTARY ON THE RANKINGS
BY DR ALOK RAY

Former Professor of Economics, Indian Institute of Management Calcutta, India where he taught for more than 30 years. He obtained his PhD from University of Rochester, USA. Prof. Ray has also taught at Calcutta University, Delhi School of Economics, Cornell University (USA), University of Rochester (USA), University of Pittsburg (USA), Portland State University (USA), Queen's University (Canada) and Monash University (Melbourne, Australia). He is the author of a book: Trade, Protection and Economic Policy (Macmillan) and many professional articles in leading international journals. In addition, he writes regular columns on contemporary issues in several English dailies. Professor Ray has been a consultant to United Nations, World Bank, Government of India and a number of private sector companies. He is a recipient of the prestigious V.K.R.V. Rao Award in Economics for his research contributions and the "Best Teacher of Economics" Award by Bengal Economic Association.

The eminent panel on Rajasthan Priorities consisted of four economists who, among themselves, had a great deal of theoretical as well as hands-on practical knowledge/experience of policymaking in India (at both central and state levels). Despite question marks over the exact BCRs and implementation/jurisdiction issues for some interventions, there was a broad general consensus about the top and the lowest priorities. The basic guiding principle was that one should try to measure the right things, even if imperfectly, than the wrong things perfectly.

Coming to our top collective consensus priorities, it is nice to see that these fell primarily in three broad areas – health, education and agriculture – all currently areas of major concern in India. For example, treatment and active case finding of Tuberculosis gets the highest ranking. Apart from the benefits in terms of lives saved of the patients directly treated, there are significant additional benefits in the form of potential lives saved of others who would have been affected by TB through the contagion effect, especially among the poor people who live in congested unhygienic conditions. The cost of treatment needed for only a few months at a stretch for complete cure, on the other hand, is very low. The problem is that cases are not detected early or treatments are not completed or proper treatments are not provided as

TB resistant to early generation drugs is not diagnosed properly. Consequently, BCR (and social desirability) is found to be very high for this intervention.

It also came out that some simple things like educating people about the benefits of hand-washing and breast feeding, providing nutrition supplements and iron tablets to women, holding immunization camps in lagging districts, diabetes screening and treatment, and community mobilization against domestic violence can buy a lot of benefits at low cost. In a sense, these are low hanging fruits which do not require any new complex or costly infrastructure (mostly needs better coordination and revamping of the existing ones) but can generate significant benefits quite easily.

Some other interventions - like expanding ambulance networks (both rural and urban) to transport emergency patients to better equipped hospitals quickly, piped drinking water supply (both urban and rural), developing/improving urban sewerage, waste water treatment and garbage collection system, and providing computer-aided teaching in schools - despite having relatively high capital and maintenance costs, have been found to have far greater social benefits.

In agriculture, establishing/strengthening E-mandis (rank 10) to reduce middlemen's margins and bring higher returns to farmers, and better quality certified seed production to increase yield (rank 12) get very high marks. In addition, building cold chains and warehouses would significantly increase farmer's income through several channels. First, it would cut down the current high rate of wastage of farm produce like milk, fruits and vegetables. Second, farmers would be able to sell their produce at higher price by choosing the appropriate timing of sales, instead of being forced to sell at low price right after the harvest. Third, they would be able to diversify towards higher value but perishable crops like fruits and flowers (that have good international as well as national markets) which is not possible without an appropriate cold chains infrastructure. Renovation of traditional water harvesting is an additional priority area, especially in a highly water deficient state like Rajasthan. Improved digitization of land records (rank 6), in addition to its other benefits, would facilitate establishing legal property rights and thus help farmers get better prices, markets, credit, high yielding seeds and scientific farming techniques through contract farming and producer's cooperatives (reaping economies of scale and higher bargaining power vis-à-vis big retailers). So, all these steps, (best) if implemented as a package, would go a long way towards improving the economic fortune of farmers who have been going through hard times.

Politically, too, farmers' distress, suicides and agitations are major issues right now. Thus, these interventions would make very good economic as well as political sense.

Family planning (rank 34, my own rank 7) is another area which should receive much greater priority than it is getting now, but for a different reason (in my judgment). Not so much for reducing the number of people (which is usually emphasized) but for improving the quality of population (less emphasized). Better educated more affluent families have already reduced the birth rate below the replacement rate while some other sections have not. If, through education and other initiatives, the fertility rate for the lagging sections can be brought down, it would provide a significant boost to per capita GDP (at both state and national levels) not simply by reducing the denominator but more significantly by raising the numerator.

At the other extreme, a few favorite projects of politicians like farm loan waiver, soil health cards, expanding crop insurance, extending solar power to more rural homes and additional free trade warehousing zones have been found to be having low BCRs.

Finally, here are some areas where I differ from the median eminent panel rankings/priorities.

In my personal judgment, it does not make sense to further extend national optical fiber network to rural areas (though it gets

38th rank in median rankings). Apart from the issues of high capital cost, possibility of theft of cables and equipments, and unreliable power supply in rural areas, the advent of mobile Wi-Fi technology is already offering better, more reliable and much cheaper internet service, even in remote villages (I am talking from first-hand experience). Similarly, we should wait sometime more before installing energy storage facility in commercial buildings (rank 9). Technology has not quite stabilized here (so far only a few countries have adopted this technology) and per unit cost may come down significantly with technological advancements (like in solar power). We should not get stuck with outdated costlier technology and leave room open to take advantage of 'leapfrogging'.

During the deliberations, a couple of things came up that merit more attention in future. One, researchers - especially on competing interventions in the same area – should be more careful about the time horizon chosen. It needs to be uniform as far as possible. Otherwise, a comparability problem arises with regard to BCRs of different interventions. In some cases, benefits (like higher earning potential) or costs (like pollution costs) continue over a long period. In such instances, BCRs can be manipulated by arbitrarily choosing cut-off dates. Second, one should check whether the interventions being considered are already underway and relevant region-specific data are available. If so, then those data would be more reliable/relevant than any derived from some pilot or case studies in some other regions or countries with different ground realities.

I would conclude by pointing to a general principle in policy intervention which is insufficiently recognized. We need to be very clear about our objective and then focus on what intervention achieves that objective most directly. Sometimes that is missed because many objectives are tried at the same time through a policy instrument which creates confusion. For instance, if preventing child marriage (i.e. before 18) is the goal, then the best intervention is to provide a cash subsidy to the girl receivable only after she attains the age of 18. Giving a subsidy in the form of bicycles or books or mid-day meals to school going girls may attain other objectives like attending school but would not necessarily postpone marriage till 18. Some say, giving lump sum cash after attaining age 18 incentivizes parents to get their daughter married right after she becomes 18. No harm if that really happens. In fact, in that case the objective of preventing early marriage has been achieved. Similarly, if attaining school degree is the objective (and not merely going to school), then the best intervention should be a cash subsidy or a bond receivable/encashable only after producing the degree certificate.

COMMENTARY ON THE RANKINGS
BY DR RATHIN ROY

Director and CEO of the National Institute of Public Finance and Policy New Delhi; and Member, Economic Advisory Council to the Prime Minister of India. With postings in London, New York, Kathmandu, Brasilia and Bangkok, he has worked as an Economic Diplomat and Policy Advisor with UNDP, focusing on emerging economies. He has taught at the Universities of Manchester and London and served as Economic Adviser with the Thirteenth Finance Commission and as a Member, Seventh Central Pay Commission, Government of India. Dr. Roy is Member, India Advisory Committee, United Nations Environment Programme (UNEP) Inquiry into a Sustainable Financial System, Member on the Meta Council on Inclusive Growth, World Economic Forum, Geneva, Member on FRBM Review Committee, Government of India. Dr. Roy's policy interests and publications have mainly focused on fiscal and macroeconomic issues pertinent to human development in developing and emerging economies. Dr. Roy has written extensively on fiscal space for human development, inter-government fiscal issues, fiscal marksmanship, macroeconomic conditionality and IMF Article-IV policy analyses. Dr. Roy holds a Ph.D in Economics from the University of Cambridge, an MA in Economics from the Jawaharlal Nehru University and a BA (Hons) in Economics from St. Stephen's College, University of Delhi.

My overall ranking was to first assess the validity of the Benefit Cost Ratio exercise. I then examined the extent to which the economic rationale provided for the exercise in the India and Rajasthan context caused the Benefit Cost Ratio to possibly overstate or understate the value for money from the intervention. I also examined the literature cited (where such literature was key in finding and/or quantifying the Benefit Cost Ratio).

The only case in which my overall ranking diverged from that of interventions ranked by BCR was that of 'Education'. This was because, in my view, the rankings relied exclusively on single source for calculation of benefits and in my view these were not easily transposable to either the India or the Rajasthan context.

Overall while my ranking differed somewhat in the middle of the spectrum, they were largely in conformance with high/low Benefit Cost Ratio ranking at the upper and lower end of the spectrum.

Comments on Top And Bottom Rankings:

I ranked 'Nutrition' as a package at number one (Rank 1-4; 7). The 'Nutrition' proposal presented five policy interventions. I was intended to demonstrate substantial benefits from delivery of nutrition based interventions. BCRs have been estimated for each individual intervention. Two of them demonstrated extremely high BCRs (43 and 37), the others, positive BCRs (6, 7, 5). It appeared to be author's contention that these interventions should be used as a package. The analytical framework indeed did take a package approach and it appeared that cherry picking individual elements of this package, including doing so by selecting those with high BCRs, would not yield maximum benefit per rupee of public expenditure. The analytical framework in the proposal/study was excellent, carefully argued and quantified the result significant both from a development impact and a value for money perspective. But, I was not convinced that the high BCRs for individual interventions justify their stand-alone ranking. Thus, I chose to rank the nutrition package as a whole at number one.

Secondly, the interventions proposed in the 'Tuberculosis' sector had attractive BCRs and they were carefully modelled with clear explanations of costs and benefits. Hence, I ranked them at number two (Rank 5-6).

In the case of the 'e-mandis', there was detailed evidence on benefits from different Indian states and a credible translation into the Rajasthan context. The calculus of costs and benefits applied to Rajasthan has been done fairly carefully. Moreover, the high BCR made me rank the intervention of 'e-mandis' at number eight.

The other top rankings included interventions like 'Secondary prevention of cardiovascular disease (CVD)' wherein, the main intervention was the administration of a drug to treat CVD which is cost effective as it dramatically reduces the need for surgical and hospital based interventions.

For the interventions which were ranked at the bottom, there were multiple reasons. For example, ‘Energy storage in commercial buildings-hybrid salts’ is an out-dated technology, ‘Farmer loan waivers’ was not a much designed intervention, in terms of either cost or benefit calculus. In other cases the interventions did not fit well in the context of Rajasthan.

NEXT STEPS

The output of Rajasthan Priorities presented in this book provide food for thought, and a valuable policy-making input. To date there has already been an incredibly encouraging response from the state government.

We were delighted that Chief Minister Hon. Vasundhara Raje found the cost-benefit approach "very interesting, an innovative methodology to spend relatively small amounts to create the most social and economic impact". She advised our team to connect with the Principal Secretary, Mr Akhil Arora, to take forward 4-5 pilots with some of the recommended interventions. She further added that if successful, the state can more systematically use benefit-to-cost analysis in all other sectors.

Dr. Jyoti Kiran, Chairperson, State Finance Commission, also warmly welcomed the research: "The Rajasthan Priorities approach of benefit-cost analysis provides very helpful insights." She demonstrated with data how the chief minister's vision matches some of the identified priorities in certain areas, and noted that Rajasthan has already made significant progress through innovative interventions. The research findings align with the state's priorities in education, poverty graduation programs, rural sanitation, water supply and irrigation, all identified as important solutions by this new process.

Chief Secretary, Hon'ble D. B. Gupta, said: "This project provides a useful methodology that the state welcomes. The state's ministries will look carefully at the research to ensure that it uses the latest data, and is finely tuned, ensuring that it will be of maximum use for Rajasthan."

Principal Secretary Akhil Arora issued a Circular, sharing the research findings and outlining the purpose of the project. The Circular requested that recipients in the state government "examine the said reports and intimate the future course of action at the earliest", and informed recipients of the Hon'ble Chief

Minister's directive that departments should examine the findings, and incorporate relevant findings into Annual Action Plans.

We are excited by the potential to continue to work closely with the state of Rajasthan, and all interested in its future, to ensure that this new data can be as helpful as possible in informing decisions that continue to boost progress.

Government of Rajasthan
Planning (Gr.-IV) Department

Sub:- Rajasthan Priorities : Finding Smart Policies using Cost Benefit Analysis.

As you are aware, Copenhagen Consensus Centre with Tata Trust conducted some cost benefit research studies under Rajasthan Priorities Project, a part of India Consensus's prioritization projects. The aim of cost-benefit analysis is to identify what delivers the higher value for money in terms of social-economic and environmental effects per rupee spend. These studies provide evidence on the costs and benefits of specific policies/interventions for State and help prioritize in terms of delivering the maximum benefits given the limited financial resources.

These research studies have already been shared with your department by Chief Secretary Office and Planning Department. Findings of these research studies were discussed in the meeting on 11th June, 2018 chaired by Chief Secretary. A meeting to share the findings of studies with Hon'ble Chief Minister was also held on 11th June, 2018. In the meeting Hon'ble Chief Minister had directed that departments should examine and the findings which are found relevant may be incorporated in Annual Action Plans.

Therefore, you are requested to examine the said reports and intimate the future course of action at the earliest.

(Akhil Arora)
Principal Secretary, Plan

Addition Chief Secretary/Pr. Secretary/Secretary,
Finance, Animal Husbandry, Industries, Social Justice, Transport, Agriculture, Medical & Health, UDH & LSG, Rural Development, Energy, PHED, Water Resources, Science & Technology, Forest & Tourism, Education, WCD, Labour and Skill Development, Food & Civil Supply

---

U.O. Note No. F.4 (2)Plan/Gr.-IV/2016
Jaipur, Dated: 14.08.2018

Copy to Ms Manorama Bakshi, Senior Adviser, India Consensus for information.

Joint Secretary, Plan

Reflections on the Findings: The Use and Utilisation of this Research

By R. Pavithra Kumar

Since the inception of Tata Trusts, the organisation has played a leading role in transforming traditional ideas of charity and introducing the concept of philanthropy to make a real difference to communities across India.

Through grant-making, direct implementation and co-partnership strategies, the Trusts support and drive innovation in a myriad of areas, including healthcare and nutrition; water and sanitation; energy; education; rural livelihoods; natural resource management; urban poverty alleviation; enhancing civil society and governance; media, arts, crafts and culture; and diversified employment.

In addition to promoting and facilitating initiatives in elementary education, Tata Trusts also award fellowships and merit scholarships to students pursuing higher studies. It grooms social scientists, cancer specialists, nuclear scientists and distinguished institutional administrators, who in turn have striven to make the country a power to reckon with in various fields, including science and technology.

The Trusts also support causes and initiatives that provide disaster relief and aids in rescue work in case of calamities. The Trusts not only assist by providing grants and helping to mobilise funds, they also offer on-ground support directly as well as in partnership with other stakeholders.

With such a broad approach, the Trusts have long had the approach of engaging with leaders in many fields, including researchers, government bodies, international agencies and like-minded private sector organisations, to nurture a self-sustaining eco-system that collectively works within every one of the areas in which the philanthropy engages.

This approach has extended to our partnership with the Copenhagen Consensus Center and with the researchers whose work is presented in this book. Tata Trusts developed and fostered these relationships with the motivation to ensure that state governments and many other interested parties are provided with cutting-edge analysis on approaches to solving the biggest challenges of today.

That is because of our enduring belief that one of the most important contributions that the Trusts can make is to significantly contribute to building intellectual capital and the knowledge base in the country.

This approach is underpinned by the belief that evidence and analysis is a crucial input to decision-making of any sort. And when it comes to philanthropy or government-spending, it is especially wise to look closely at what each rupee achieves, to maximise the returns to society and ensure that investment leads to results.

This project has, to date, produced research that allows for insights that can lead to better-informed decision-making.

It is an important principle that the Trusts share this knowledge freely with other philanthropies, corporations, researchers, government organisations, and—perhaps most importantly--state governments across India.

Ensuring that relevant state governments can avail themselves of this research is just one step in a multifaceted program of engagement that includes providing technical support, along with adapting and updating this research to ensure that it can best and most meaningfully be utilised.

State governments are in many ways the engine room of India's future progress, so it is crucial that they are fully empowered with the evidence and knowledge to make well-informed decisions.

We are very heartened and encouraged by the Rajasthan planning department advising its various state departments to act on the priorities and by the request from the Andhra Pradesh Chief

Minister for an action plan based on the research presented in this book.

The research presented in this book, whether on how to build educational outcomes, improve health results, lift economic performance, or enhance environmental wellbeing, contains such evidence that, collectively or individually, can be taken up by state governments, and other organisations, to be utilised in ways that improve the decision-making process.

An additional important potential audience is to be found within the private sector of India. Through corporate social responsibility (CSR) programmes, businesses can be at the forefront of finding ways to make a positive difference within the communities they inhabit and work alongside.

Innovative CSR has great potential to enhance community wellbeing, owing to enabling government legislation that has created the ecosystem for proper engagement. It is important, though, that CSR funds are spent just as wisely as any other money spent by a business, in order to ensure that this is sustainable and / or meaningful.

For those working in this space, looking carefully at the findings presented by this project, whether within a topic or across all subjects, can be a very fruitful starting point for prudent CSR management.

With close to 1,000 + projects being executed through 700+ partners, Tata Trusts reached millions of households across India. This is a broad remit, meaning that knowledge generation and sharing, from one community and state to another, is at the heart of developing a knowledge base that can be usefully applied.

This research can enhance that mission, and can be utilised in ways that will ensure that lessons are learned from success stories around India—and to applying those lessons wisely.

R. Pavithra Kumar
Director – Program Design, Tata Trusts

Made in the USA
Monee, IL
04 November 2026

67382295R00075